P.

SEX AND THE OVER-FORTIES

Also by Robert Chartham and available in the NEL series

SEX MANNERS FOR MEN
SEX MANNERS FOR ADVANCED LOVERS
SEX MANNERS FOR THE YOUNG GENERATION

SEX and the OVER-FORTIES

Robert Chartham

NEW ENGLISH LIBRARY
TIMES MIRROR

First published in Great Britain by Leslie Frewin Ltd in 1969

*

FIRST NEL EDITION APRIL 1971

*

NEL Books are published by
New English Library Limited from Barnard's Inn, Holborn, London, E.C.1.
Made and printed in Great Britain by Hunt Barnard Printing Ltd., Aylesbury, Bucks.

45000828 2

Contents

1: On Passing into Middle-age

As we tend, by the advancement of science, to live longer than our forefathers, it becomes increasingly difficult to define what we mean by middle-age. In the sixteenth and seventeenth centuries a man was old at fifty; in Victorian times old-age crept up at sixty; our grandfathers were old at seventy. The number of sprightly seventy-fives and eighties of my father's generation who, within the knowledge of most of us, negotiate busy roads, walk four or five miles a day, engage in quite heavy gardening or pursuits which demand a lively intellect, seems to indicate that we, all things being equal, have a chance of warding off senility at least until the age of eighty-five.

Strictly speaking, then, middle-age should begin somewhere around forty to forty-five. But it doesn't work quite like that. Men of forty these days are, on the whole, vigorous, healthy and strong, not yet perhaps even at the peak of their intellectual powers. For it seems that the longer senility is kept at bay, the longer we sustain our full physical and mental activities.

It is not really possible to define middle-age. There comes a time, however, between forty-five and fifty-five, when we become aware that activities which we have carried out without conscious effort now require a deliberate act of will to perform. We begin to tire physically much more easily and the mental effort required to carry out our normal mental tasks is greatly increased.

The first realisation that this is happening to us invariably produces a shock; not a shock of such dimensions that treatment is needed to counteract it; but nevertheless a mental reaction which requires a definite conscious effort of will to restore the former peace of mind. But why do we experience such a shock? The truth is that we all fear old-age.

Man is a psychologically complicated animal, and his fear of old-age is derived from many sources of apprehension. Old-age, for instance, means that death is approaching. (When shall we, I wonder, be able to accept calmly the inevitability of death instead of creating in our minds a screen to block it out of our consciousness?) Or again, old-age can mean the experience of failing physical powers to the extent of personal suffering through disease due to the malfunctioning of wearing-out or worn-out organs; which, in turn, means that we shall be reliant to some degree or other on the ministrations of others. Few of us are not endowed with a self-pride in which self-reliance plays a large part. The very thought that we cannot look after ourselves completely is enough to cause shudders of self-revulsion to run down our spines. 'I've always stood on my own two feet and . . . and . . . ' We hesitate and trail off because we dare not, in honesty to ourselves, maintain that we shall be able to do so for the rest of our lives.

Or again, old-age means retirement. The number of us who plan ahead for retirement is fantastically small, which is another indication of our refusal to face up to the facts of life. The horror of retirement springs from the fact that our working lives not only take up the greater part of our existence, but that this large chunk of our lives is organised for us by the routine and exigencies of our jobs. The vast vacuum which ceasing to do our jobs will create in our day-to-day existence will have to be filled by our own efforts, and we have little or no experience of the practical side of organising activites required to take up several hours a day.

The prospect of old-age, then, can be quite a terrifying one from several points of view – from the physical, by reason of organic deterioration with its attendant illnesses and handicaps, and from the psychological, by reason of the average individual's lack of mental equipment to fill prolonged leisure. What is needed is a moral fibre which accepts the inevitability of old-age before it overtakes one, and provides a drive which makes it possible to prepare ahead for old-age.

Generally speaking, the first warning of old-age comes at the onset of middle-age. It is at this period in time that one ought to begin to come to terms with the idea of growing old and to think, at least, about planning for the distant future.

But it is precisely at this point that by far the greater number of men begin to adopt an ostrich-head-in-the-sand attitude not only towards old-age, but towards middle-age itself. It is now that they make their greatest mistake, for if middle-age is faced realistically, there will be automatically no fear of old-age.

As I have said, it is not possible to define the limits of middle-age. Strictly speaking, middle-age begins when the peak of full maturity has passed. I am speaking now of physical maturity. The age at which the peak of full maturity is reached – that is to say, when all the organs are functioning at their best – depends on a number of factors. I have never seen it alluded to anywhere, but it would be interesting to know how many babies at the moment of birth are physically completely perfect; or how many children who have imperfections reach their peak of maturity physically completely perfect.

It seems to me that physical maturity is a very individual thing. There is a period in everyone's life when all organs are functioning at the height of their capacity. This goes for those organs which were slightly imperfect at the moment of birth, and which have never reached a state of full perfection. But the man who reaches this functional climax, though some of his organs are not functioning absolutely perfectly, has as much right to claim to have reached physical maturity as the completely perfect physical specimen, every one of whose organs from the moment of birth has functioned with absolute perfection.

After the climax of maturity an inexorable process of degeneration sets in. The rate of degeneration, too, is an individual factor. At the apex is, of course, the perfect physical specimen whose organs, because they have functioned perfectly, have a slower speed of degeneration than those of individuals who have had a slight malfunctioning of one or two organs from birth. At the base is the man who has had a multi-organ malfunctioning from birth.

The human body, however, is such a complicated machine

that for practical purposes we have to disregard the perfect. We must take the average if we are to make any sense at all of Man's experience of living. Even then, there are many shadings of the average, and to make any progress we have to reduce this, too, to three broad types – those who accept that they have passed the peak of physical maturity; those who realise that they have passed the peak of physical maturity but who refuse to accept it; and those who, having realised that they have passed the peak of physical maturity, have no interest whatsoever in trying to compensate for their progressive degeneration.

Type A I accept as the norm. By category A's reactions I judge the reactions of types B and C. Type A can cope admirably with his own problems, and needs little or no help from anyone. Types B and C, however, are the people who need to be talked to, and it is to them, and especially to type C, that I would like to address this book.

Let us consider type B first in very general terms. One day, having run for his train, he throws himself into his seat and all of a sudden realises that his heart is thumping wildly, he is breathing heavily and sweat is trickling down his forehead. He has run a hundred or a hundred and fifty yards; and that is a terrible thing. A year or eighteen months ago he could have run that distance and not noticed it. A friend sitting opposite looks across and smiles, 'Getting old, eh? It comes to us all!'

Or, for two or three consecutive days he has had to work late at the office. At the end of the three days, he suddenly realises how very tired he is. A year or eighteen months ago, though he would have been weary, perhaps, he would not have had this awful feeling of exhaustion that he has now. After supper he falls asleep in front of the television. At bedtime his wife wakes him up and, ashamed, he apologises. 'Never mind, dear,' she consoles him, 'you've been working so hard, and you're not so young as you were.'

Or, he and his wife are asked to a dinner-dance, beginning at eight and finishing at two. It is three before they get to bed. Next morning he prepares for the day feeling as tired as if he hadn't had any sleep at all, and an ache in his calves and thighs and the small of his back indicates only too clearly how out of condition he is. A year ago they used to go dancing now and again, and he never used to feel like this next day, even after only three or four hours' sleep. The reminder suddenly makes him realise that 'he can't do what he did'.

The transition from energetic activity *without* after-effects to such activity *with* after-effects is so gradual that one is not aware that one's physical capabilities are deteriorating. It is very like weight. The awareness that one has put on weight is also a sudden experience. The extra ounces are added so slowly that not until the trouser-band becomes so tight, or the waist of the dress so constricting, that it forces itself on one's consciousness, does one realise that one has, in fact, put on pounds, if not stones, in the last six months.

In whatever way the awareness that middle-age has crept up is discovered, type B reacts to it with firmness and determination. He rejects the truth, or if he accepts it, pushes it back into the dark recesses of his mind, and deliberately forgets about it. He pretends to himself that it is not middle-age that has crept up on him, but that he has been slack about exercise and diet. He will soon put that right, he promises himself, and he embarks on a programme of physical exercises far beyond his capabilities, which, every now and again, has serious and sometimes fatal consequences.

Certainly exercise in moderation, and an eye on the diet and on drinking, are admirable antidotes to the swift encroachment of degeneration. But too strenuous exercise, like no exercise at all, will only hasten the process. What is needed is a nice sense of balance, and to acquire an intelligent approach, which is how type A deals with the situation.

Type C has middle-age brought to his consciousness in much the same way as type B. However, having realised that he is now in middle-age, he takes refuge in inactivity. He says to himself, 'I'm middle-aged and soon I will be old. This is inevitable. There is nothing I can do about it, so why worry? I'll just let nature take its course.' From then on, life becomes a bore. Often he accepts even the boredom and grows into a crabby, disillusioned old man, with a grudge against himself and those around him, and against life as a whole.

Now, there is one aspect of living that becomes noticeably

affected by the advancing years. I mean, of course, one's sexual activity. Except in quite exceptional cases – though there are, thank heavens, plenty of these about – the sex-drive and the physical reactions of the sexual system are among the casualties of general degeneration.

So far I have made no reference to women and middle-age, except in one very brief passing reference to waist-bands of dresses. What I have said about men and their discovery of middle-age can often be applied to women, but somehow or other, the discovery never seems quite so suddenly thrust upon them. A woman reaches the conclusion by a more gradual process and, though she can be classified into types A, B, and C, which conform reactionwise to the male types, the way she copes with her situation is different; except, possibly, in the case of type C.

It is in one aspect of her sexual life, however, that she has middle-age thrust upon her in a way which she can do nothing to counteract. She cannot delay the process of changing from a fertile, child-bearing woman into a barren woman incapable of bearing children. The process of the menopause is as inexorable as old age and death. The permanent cessation of ovulation and menstruation is a milestone in *every* woman's life. The process by which it is brought about – some time between the ages of forty-five and fifty-five – is a complex one in which tremendous organic and secretion changes are involved. On the other hand, once the changes have been completed, she is still not only capable of accepting the penis and going through the motions of coupling, she is also capable of a positive response through to orgasm and is subject to a sex-drive which can be as strong as it was while she was capable of fulfilling her reproductive function. In fact, as I shall be explaining later, the release from the fear of unwanted pregnancy can be of such dimensions that after she has passed the menopause she very often achieves sustained sexual experience of a quality she never achieved in her middle twenties, at the peak of her sexual potential.

A man has not this definite sexual milestone to delineate his entry into middle-age. Some authorities maintain, though, in my view on very flimsy evidence, that men undergo a kind of menopause. They say that certain glandular changes take place in men which produce symptoms similar to those experienced by women when going through the menopause – heart-pounding, restlessness, headaches, depressions, irritability, becoming easily exhausted, and hot and cold flushes. If a man does have these symptoms in middle-age, they are certainly not so marked as in women; and they are certainly not experienced by *all* men. After a certain age, the semen may contain sub-standard spermatozoa incapable of fertilising the egg, or even no spermatozoa at all; the Cowper's glands' secretion may progressively become less in volume and disappear altogether after a time; the volume of semen ejaculated may become less, though it rarely dries up completely; and it is true that the prostate and testicles become markedly changed; but none of these things is such an effective end to reproduction as the menopause is for the woman. There are many men who, while experiencing a slackening off of the sex-drive, are still capable of producing healthy children in their sixties and seventies.

The man's greatest and permanent fear is that he will lose the ability to have an erection, that is, become impotent. Erection, not fatherhood, is the true test of a man's manhood, which is closely supported, not by his ability to produce fine high standard spermatozoa, but by his ability to have a firm upstanding erection and to sustain it for a period far longer than is necessary sexually to satisfy his wife, or ideally, as he grows older, a girl half his age. It is the threat to his virility which old-age is reputed to be that, in the sexual sector of his life, produces the shock reaction of middle-age. He will gladly admit to being incapable of running for the train without experiencing physical exertion, or to being exhausted by two hours' fairly heavy gardening, but the thought of not being able to couple with a sexual partner and satisfy her is too horrible to contemplate; or, should impotence overtake him, too final to do anything about.

Type B, in the same way that he rejects the onset of middle-age by changing into shorts as soon as he gets home and running three miles before supper, or indulging in strenuous squash or tennis, goes haywire in his sexual life. His wife is not a sufficient sexual challenge to him, and he has to prove that his powers of seduction and love-making are in no degree diminishing by embarking on a round of promiscuity with young girls of half his age, or any mature woman foolish enough to pop into bed with him. His attempts to prove to *himself* that he is a modern Casanova often lead him more deeply into difficulties than if he transformed himself into a type C; for, if his wife discovers his wanderings from the marriage-bed and does not understand what is really happening to him, she may, as indeed she is entitled to, sue him for divorce, or else, while not going to this extreme, exclude him from her sexual life. Not only this, if he does actually indulge in sexual-physical excesses he may, after a time, find that the shock to his sexual system that the unwonted activity has caused has engendered irregularities of response in the form of premature ejaculation, intermittent total impotence, or a form of permanent semi-impotence. Or he may find at the outset that he is more active in the breach than in the performance – a condition brought about by psychological barriers, which he automatically erects, generally unconsciously, when he attempts to move out of his customary ethical environment. If he does find himself at any time unable to complete intercourse, and the condition persists, he goes even more haywire, pawing, patting and pinching and indulging in what he believes is titillating talk, which impresses no one but himself and earns for him the reputation of being a dirty old man.

That he should behave like this is not due one hundred per cent to his own aberrations. Were his wife sexually adequate and willing to accept his sudden excess of sexual activity, he would not become an errant Don Juan, though he might flirt with other women, just to prove that his magnetism did in fact still exist. But one of the unfortunate concomitants of this type of middle-aged compensatory sexual behaviour is a sexual partner who has let middle-age overwhelm her. The run-to-seed wife also sets in motion her own compensating mechanism. Very often this takes the form of making the menopause, or rather the onset of the menopause with its attendant aches and pains and irregularities, the excuse for initially becoming sexually lazy, and then for withdrawing from sexual experience altogether on the grounds that it is undignified for a woman of fifty-five or so to admit to enjoying sex still.

While I hate to say so, where sex becomes a problem or a has-been in more cases than not it is the wife's response to middle-age that is one of the major factors in bringing about what is, in my view, little short of tragedy. For let me declare my interest even at this early stage: if approaching sixty, I really believed, or could imagine, that in ten, fifteen or twenty years' time, given reasonably good health, I shall not still be enjoying sex as I did when a young husband of twenty-one and am doing so even more, nearly forty years later, half my reason for living would disappear. I cannot visualise what life without sex must be like at any period of one's existence. It has given me more joy and consolation, more happiness and contentment than I have derived from any other experience except my wife's companionship, and even that is based upon our continuing sexual rapport. If this can happen to us, I cannot see why it should not also be the experience of any couple, each within the sexual pattern which they have found in early married life most suited them.

Again unfortunately, the woman more often than not contributes to the terrible sexual lethargy which chiefly characterises type C. I shall be dealing with this type in much greater detail in Chapter 4, and all I will say now is that these people take the line of least resistance. Something has gone wrong at some stage of their development as mistresses and lovers. Somewhere along the line they have found sex a bore. In my books *Sex Manners for Men* and *Mainly for Wives* I have worked not only on the assumption, but on the proven facts, that a satisfactory, well-attuned sex-life in marriage is the cement which holds together the many bricks of which marriage is built – trust, affection, sympathy, understanding, love, the combined confrontation of the many practical difficulties which beset a marriage, the tremendous companionship which evolves from the crises weathered together, the happy moments shared and so on. Sex activity between husband and wife, I have said again and again, is the visible, concrete expression of love. By the thought and care which a couple devote to their love-play, their coupling and their mutual gratitude for the experienced ecstasy may be judged the quality of their love for one another.

At the outset of marriage emotional love is *the* prime ingredient of the couple's new joint-life together. This love they try to express in the intimate relationship of physical sex. In a marriage that is well founded the sexual expression of love should not deteriorate; it should, indeed, develop and burgeon the deeper the relationship becomes.

Conversely, if the sexual relationship breaks down at middle-age, then it is practically certain that the couple have not been deeply involved with emotional and physical sex. By 'not deeply involved' I mean they have not made any or much attempt to improve their technique of love-making much, if at all, beyond the basic requirements for relieving sexual tension - rousing the woman in fore-play so that she comes off at some time during the act, and putting the penis in the vagina and moving it about until ejaculation occurs. They have not tried to improve their orgasmic experience, probably because they never knew that techniques of foreplay and coupling exist which can greatly intensify the sensations at climax. They have made love, or rather, they have had sex – because love has not really come into their sexual experience at all – merely in response to the sex-drive or one or the other, and have not dignified the physical process by making it the visible symbol of emotional love. Their enjoyment of sex has been simply in the pleasurable sensations of orgasm and the tension-relieved aftermath; they have not had any joy from their love-making, because they have not deliberately made it an occasion for joy.

I have been talking and writing about sex long enough to realise that having said these things I shall be accused of generalisation. I am well aware of the ease with which one can generalise especially in sexual matters, but this time I have the records of some original research to back me up. A short time ago 174 men and 136 women, married and over the age of fifty, completed a questionnaire of 87 questions which I put to them, on the most intimate side of their sexual lives. Those who were sexually active and clearly enjoyed their love-making had invariably taken trouble with their sex-lives from the first days of marriage; while those who hardly made love to their partners, or grumbled about their partner's withdrawal from sex – all too often, complete withdrawal – had invariably used their sexual experience, as I have described above, merely for relief from sexual tension; or had been content for the man to mount the woman in the orthodox western position – and no other – purely to satisfy their sex-drive. In the final section I have given some facts and figures, and some case-histories, from the material provided by these questionnaires, and there you will find statistics and evidence which support my contention.

As I said earlier, it is chiefly to those over fifty who have, to all intents and purposes, 'given up sex,' 'dropped out of sex,' or have run into difficulties when they make the occasional attempt at love-making, that I would like to address this book. After all, it is a waste of time to preach to the converted, and according to my figures, they are a very large group indeed. This I find distressing.

I find it distressing because the sexually-disinterested over-fifty, the middle-aged drop-out from sex, practically automatically has several gaps in the overall marriage relationship. You may take it for certain that where there is an undoubted deep companionship between a middle-aged or elderly married couple, there will also be a deeply satisfying sexual relationship. And the converse is equally true. Where it is obvious to the onlooker that the marriage relationship is nothing more than an arrangement of convenience – based on financial security for the woman and the provision of an unpaid housekeeper for the man – the sex-relationship will be either wholly non-existent, or where it does exist, be wholly or partially unsatisfactory to both partners. They have not the intimacy of companionship to colour their lives; they have dispensed with love; and they lack even the fleeting intimacy of sex to give at least some meaning to their existence. This was not what they married for. They have failed as marriage partners, they are failures as men and women.

The tragedy is that it need not happen. Middle-age, if approached intelligently, far from being the beginning of the end can open up brand new experiences. It can be the time when a couple start to consolidate all they have learned of life and living in their first half-century. By this time they have grown to know – or should have grown to know – exactly what makes their partner tick. On the basis of this knowledge they can found a way of life that is calm and fulfilling, in which mutual confidence becomes the fount of mutual happiness. In this new experience of living, sex has a definite – and major – role to play.

2: What Happens When You Make Love

In the past few weeks I have had the opportunity of asking three men and three women in their middle fifties how much they knew about the physical side of love. Among the questions I asked were:

1 What happens to make the penis erect?
2 Is the penis naturally lubricated?
3 Does a woman come every time she makes love?
4 What is the man's most sexually sensitive spot?
5 What is the woman's most sexually sensitive spot?
6 What are the man's other sexually sensitive spots?
7 What are the woman's other sexually sensitive spots?
8 A man can come within two to five minutes of direct stimulation of his erect penis. How long does it take the average woman?
9 A man and woman usually perform the sexual act by the man lying above the woman, putting his penis into her vagina and moving it backwards and forwards until he comes. Are there any other positions for intercourse?
10 When a man is sexually stimulated his penis becomes erect. How does a woman react physically to sexual stimulation?
11 Do you or your partner ever discuss physical sex?

By the way, I knew that none of the six had ever read a sex-manual.

The answers I received illustrate, I think, that the number of men and women in their fifties today, who have what I like to call a reasonable working-knowledge of their own and their partner's sexual responses, is much lower than one would expect it to be in the age of the permissive society. They also show that some men and women of the First World War generation, who have spent the whole of their lives in the so-called era of sexual emancipation, have been able to contract out and let the greater sexual freedom pass by them.

These were the replies:

What happens to make the penis erect?

MEN: One man had no idea. The other two said they had heard that it was caused by the increased blood-flow, but only one knew that the penis was composed of spongy tissue.

WOMEN: Two did not know, though one of them suggested that the penis was a mass of nerves which grew taut when the man was sexually stimulated. The third said she *thought* it was caused by blood. When I asked her how, she said she believed there was a large hollow space running through the length of the interior of the penis, and it was this that filled with blood.

Is the penis naturally lubricated?

MEN: Two said yes. The third said no, if he was anything to go by.

WOMEN: Two did not know. The third said she believed so, because sometimes when she felt her husband's penis before he went into her, it 'was all slippery'.

Does a woman come every time she makes love?

MEN: One had no idea; one didn't see why she shouldn't; the third said he didn't think so, because sometimes his wife got very excited, but at other times didn't seem to have any response at all.

WOMEN: All three said no, judging by their own experience, and if they could be reckoned as average women.

What is the man's most sexually sensitive spot?

MEN: All three said the tip of the penis just below the

opening.

WOMEN: All three said the penis. When I asked if they meant the whole of it, all three said yes.

What is the woman's most sexually sensitive spot?

MEN: All three said they *supposed* the interior of the vagina was. Only one had heard of the clitoris, but he could not describe it or its site.

WOMEN: All three said the entrance to the vagina and the clitoris, though they didn't call it that.

What are the man's other sexually sensitive spots?

MEN: Two said they hadn't any, but the third said he found the pressure of his wife's hands on his buttocks after he had gone into her very exciting.

WOMEN: One said her husband seemed to enjoy it when she fondled his scrotum gently; another said her husband liked to have his back stroked; the third said she did not think men had any sensitive spots other than the penis.

What are the woman's other most sexually sensitive spots?

MEN: All three said the breasts, and particularly the nipples. One said the entrance of the vagina stimulated by a finger or fingers.

WOMEN: All three said breasts, nipples, thighs, navel (to stimulation of tongue-tip), throat and shoulders.

How long does it take the average woman to come?

MEN: No idea.

WOMEN: All three said much longer than two to five minutes. One thought that at least twenty minutes of foreplay was essential.

Are there any other positions for intercourse besides the face-to-face-man-above?

MEN: All three mentioned face-to-face woman above, and a side position. One mentioned rear-entry on sides, but thought it 'rather daring'.

WOMEN: All three mentioned face-to-face-woman-above,

one face-to-face-on-chair, one rear-entry-woman-kneeling.

How does a woman react physically to sexual stimulation?

MEN: All three said the vaginal entrance swells and the nipples become hard.
WOMEN: All said the vagina entrance swells and the nipples become hard.

Do you and your partner ever discuss physical sex?

MEN: Two said no, definitely not; the third said sometimes they talk about young people having sex. Once his wife asked if she might measure his penis, because she did not believe she could receive seven inches, which he had told her it was in response to her question.
WOMEN: All said no, though two said they wished they could.

You will see from these replies that my three men and three women had the minimum basic knowledge to engage in coupling. From the answers I thought I perceived that they all engaged in some form of love-play, but I decided I should confirm this, so I put to them the following additional questions and received these replies:

Does your partner fondle you or do you fondle your partner, before the penis is put into the vagina?

MEN: One man said no: as soon as he was fully erect he and his partner began intercourse. This was the man who had previously said that he had no idea whether or not a woman comes every time she makes love. The man who said he didn't see why she shouldn't, replied to this question that he fondled his partner's breasts with his mouth for a few minutes, felt to see if the vagina entrance had swollen, and if it had, put his penis into the vagina straightaway.

The third who said that his wife got very excited on some occasions but seemed not to be aroused on others, replied that he played with his wife's nipples with his fingers, then when they had become hard, sucked them while he gently rubbed her vagina entrance with his fingers.

The first man said that his partner did not fondle him.

The others said that theirs massaged the penis in the customary masturbatory fashion.

WOMEN: All three said that their partners fondled their nipples briefly; two said that their vaginal entrances were occasionally manipulated when their partner seemed more than usually roused; one said that her husband stimulated her clitoris.

All three briefly fondled the partner's penis.

How long do you spend on this initial fondling?

MEN: Two said three or four minutes.

WOMEN: All said it didn't seem long. They were rarely fully roused. The woman who said that her husband stimulated her clitoris also said that these were the only times she reached a climax.

It seemed possible to draw another inference from these answers, so I asked:

Don't you wish your partner would fondle you more before beginning intercourse?

MEN: The man who began intercourse without any preliminaries at all gave a quite definite no; he felt he was not missing anything and his partner had never complained. The other two admitted that it had occurred to them that a more lengthy fore-play might produce greater satisfaction. One said that the older he got he had difficulties enough in controlling his progress towards coming, and he felt that if fore-play were prolonged he might come within seconds of going into his partner. (This tendency to premature ejaculation is a temporary defect of quite a number of middle-aged men. I shall be saying something about it later.)

WOMEN: All said they would like prolonged fore-play because they felt 'they might come more often as a result'.

I have quoted this mini-survey at some length because I know from experience that the approach of these six to practical sex is the approach of many. I am quite sure that if a really exhaustive survey were made, the number of men and women who have this almost superficial sex-life would shock you if you knew. It is all very well for sociologists, sexologists and others to say that the realisation by women that they were not only capable of orgasm but should demand it as of right produced a tremendous sexual revolution in the 1920s and 1930s; that men began to see themselves as failures as lovers if they did not satisfy (though orgasm) the sex-drive of their partners; and that this realisation had produced a far healthier attitude towards sex. While this is undoubtedly true for the majority, I am coming more to the opinion that the size of this majority over the minority of those represented by my sextet is only just sufficiently larger to enable it to be a majority.

Ever since I began talking and writing on practical sex, I have consistently stressed two points. First, that both partners should extract from their bodies, when they make love, the most intensely, voluptuously ecstatic sensations of which their bodies are capable. One should not be content to seek a lessening of tension by orgasm achieved in the shortest time by the most direct methods of stimulation. The higher the intensity of the orgasmic sensations the greater is the physical relief: that is an irrefutable fact. But the technique required to acquire the maximum degree of response both lifts human physical sex out of the realms of animality by making it the supreme tangible symbol of the love of the partners for one another that is the only justification for love-making that is not deliberately planned for making a baby. Second, that to acquire the maximum responses the couples must know how their own and their partners' sexual bodies work.

I do not want to mount one of my hobby-horses here about the sex instinct - my argument that though the desire to couple is instinctive, the mechanics of coupling are not and must be acquired by watching a practical demonstration or by being told or reading about how it is done.[1] But it is quite certain that the

[1] I have the impression that I may be in a minority of one in holding such views, but nevertheless I obstinately persist in them.

techniques of love-making cannot be acquired, except in those very very rare cases of what one might term inspired sexual imaginations, which work out *for themselves*, relying solely on the basic knowledge that the penis must be put into the vagina. For advanced techniques of love-making, the average couple must be told that the woman requires longer stimulation than the man, the erogenous (sensitive) zones of both must be detailed, indications of the best methods of stimulation of each zone must be given and they must have described for them at least half-a-dozen alternatives to the customary western posture of face-to-face-man-above. On this basic information, if they have the slightest imagination, they can build a technique of love-making that can draw forth sexual responses that will give a special quality to the whole marriage relationship.

Until the time comes when instruction in the techniques of love-making is compulsory; or at second best, such instruction is made readily available in the senior forms of comprehensive schools for those whose parents and guardians have no objection to their wards being taught the craft of love - along with contraceptive techniques - the individual man and woman is left to his or her devices. But for them there is at the present time only one source of such information that is at all reliable - the sex-manual. Happily there are strong indications that the availability of this source is appreciated by the younger people, at least, in significant numbers. I can say this with some authority because my own two sex-manuals, *Mainly for Wives* and *Sex Manners for Men*, have sold in large numbers and have obviously found many, many people eager to learn more about and improve their love-making.

But what goes for our children does not go for us. Far too many of our generation - the fifty- to sixty-year-olds - have been content with the minimum of sexual knowledge on which to base their sexual lives. The survey to which I referred earlier enables me to say that in those cases where sexual life after fifty is practically nonexistent, neither one of the couple has taken the trouble to develop a sexual technique which has provided a sexual experience so worthwhile that there is a wish to prolong it. In other words, the unsatisfactory - even, in many cases, nonexistent - sex-life after fifty is an inevitable outcome of a disregard in earlier years of acquiring a knowledge of sex on which a satisfactory technique could be erected.

If some of my readers have never read a sex-manual, or glanced through one so long ago that they have forgotten what it was about, I strongly suggest that they should buy one as soon as possible and read it carefully. There is a long list to choose from that are readily available, some better than others. At the risk of being immodest I would like to recommend my own two books, chiefly because, in them, according to the reviewers, I have succeeded in what I set out to do – describe sex in the ordinary straightforward language of everyday use, instead of in the pseudo-medical and quasi-scientific jargon which most other authors of sex-manuals use.

However, as I shall have to refer throughout the rest of this book to the sex apparatus and its functions of both partners, it will be convenient if I describe them very briefly here.

The man's chief sex-member is his *penis*, which hangs between his legs at the base of his belly. The penis, which varies in length and thickness from man to man - the dimensions of the average erect penis are five-and-a-half to six inches in length measured along the upper side and four-and-a-quarter inches in circumference at the base - is composed of a tissue which is full of little holes like a sponge. The head of the penis is shaped rather like an acorn, and where it joins the shaft of the penis it has a rim which very slightly protrudes from the shaft on the top side. This head is covered by a hood of loose skin, known as the foreskin, which can be pulled right back to the rim so as to expose the head. If the man is circumcised, this foreskin has been removed by a surgical operation usually within a few days of birth, and the head of the penis is always completely exposed.

The shaft of the penis is covered with ordinary skin. The head, however, has a covering of a special membrane, which is much more sensitive than ordinary skin in men who have not been circumcised. But even the membrane of the circumcised penis-head retains much of its sensitive quality throughout life.

The penis, which is outside the body, represents only two-thirds of the organ's total length. The other third, referred to as the root, is inside the body.

Behind the limp penis hangs a bag of skin called the *scrotum*. Inside the scrotum are two hard egg-shaped balls known as the *testicles*. Each testicle is made up of many yards of minute, continuous tubing, and it is in this tubing that the male sperms are produced. As they mature, the sperms pass out of the testicles into a kind of sac fixed to the top of each testicle, called the *epididymis*, and are stored there until they leave the body. From each epididymis runs a tube known as the *vas deferens*, along which the sperms pass into two reservoirs, one on either side of the bladder. These *seminal vesicles*, as they are called, produce a fluid, contact with which makes the sperms, which up to then have been somewhat sluggish, wildly active. Shaped rather like a tadpole with a broad, pointed head to which a long tail is attached, as soon as they enter the seminal fluid they begin to lash violently with their tails, which sends them scurrying hither and thither.

From the seminal vesicles the vasa deferentia continue down into the *prostate*, a gland situated at the base of the bladder. The prostate also secretes a fluid (the prostatic fluid). The *urethra*, the tube by which the urine is drawn off from the bladder, enters the prostate at the top, and leaves it at the bottom, passing down into the penis, through the whole length of which it runs to the opening in the penis-head.

When the seminal fluid leaves the vesicles with its load of sperms it mixes with the prostatic fluid. Seminal fluid prostatic fluid sperms are known as semen. This is the milky-like substance which is spurted from the opening of the penis when the man comes off, or ejaculates, at the peak of his climax. The average healthy male produces between three and five millilitres (between half and a full teaspoon) of semen at each ejaculation. In this comparatively small quantity there are about four hundred million sperms, only *one* of which is required to fertilise the egg of the female.

The penis of the man who is not sexually roused is soft and hangs limply down over the scrotum. It is very soft to the touch. It is supplied with its own system of veins and arteries which is huge compared with the system for the rest of the body. When the man is sexually stimulated, blood rushes into the penis by one set of veins and arteries and fills up all the tiny holes. Since the blood returns to the general blood-stream by the other set of arteries and veins at a much slower speed than it enters the penis, the effect is to make the penis swell and become hard and to lift it up from its limp downwards-hanging posture until it stands out from the body above the scrotum. Normally the angle of the penis with the body when it is erect is about forty-five degrees, but at least up to middle-age and very often beyond, if the man is highly excited, it may become so erect that the head taps against the belly, even when the man is standing up. Generally speaking, the erect penis is one-third longer and one-third fatter than the limp penis.

Erection is brought about in two ways. The first is by direct stimulation of one of the man's chief sensitive zones. The most sensitive of all his erogenous zones is the penis itself; and within the penis there are zones more sensitive than others. The penis-head is packed with nerves, especially round the ridge, in the tip around the opening, and most concentrated of all in the *frenum* or *frenulum*. The frenum is a small band of ordinary skin which joins the skin of the penis-shaft to the membrane covering the penis-head on the underside a little below the opening of the urethra. The nerves with which it is crammed are not only connected with the nerves which trigger off the increased blood supply to the penis, which brings about an erection, but also to the nerves which produce the *orgasm* or *climax*. In other words, if the penis-head and frenum are stimulated with the fingers - or in some other way - when the penis is limp, these nerves will cause the penis to become erect; and if this stimulation is continued after erection has taken place, in between two and five minutes the nerves prompt the muscles around the root of the penis and the prostate to contract and relax, and force the semen into the urethra, up the penis and out at the tip.

The skin covering the shaft of the penis is also a sensitive zone after the penis has become erect, though it does have a degree of sensitivity if the limp penis is fondled by someone other than the owner. As a matter of fact this is true of all the man's sensitive zones except the penis-head. A man can bring himself off, *i.e.* bring himself to orgasm, by stimulating the tip of the penis and frenum with his fingers, but he responds hardly at all to self-stimulation of the insides of his thigh, his navel, his buttocks, his throat and shoulders, or even his scrotum, which, after the penis-head, is his next most sensitive zone.

These other sensitive zones, including the scrotum, are sensitive enough to produce an erection if they are stroked or fondled or licked by some other person. Continued stimulation of them, however, after erection has taken place will not bring the man off - only stimulation of the penis-head and shaft will do that - though such stimulation will add greatly to his voluptuous sensations which gradually increase until they reach their peak with the first, second, and sometimes the third, spurt of semen from the penis.

The second way in which erection is produced is psychological. The sight of a beautiful woman, even the memory of the sight of a beautiful woman, erotic thoughts, erotic photographs and pictures, the reading of erotic passages or listening to erotic talk or taking part in it, will all cause erection without any of the sensitive zones, even the penis, being caressed and stimulated at all. In this case, the compartment of the brain which receives this mental stimulation sends messages down the pith of the spine to what is known as the *erection centre*. The erection centre is situated in the region of the spine somewhere about the small of the back. It is a sort of junction-box, where all the various branches of the sexual nervous system meet. The message, having reached the erection centre, is passed by it to those nerves which increase the flow of blood to the penis and cause it to stiffen into erection. Psychological stimulation *alone* very, very rarely, and then generally only in young people with very vivid imaginations or a high degree of sexual sensitivity, brings the man off.

Stimulation of the orgasm-producing nerves in the penis-tip is, therefore, the essential factor in bringing the man off. After erection has been established stimulation of these special nerves is embarked upon, and after a time the man begins to have the most pleasant sensations. These sensations continue to mount the longer the stimulation is applied, until a certain point is reached when the *involuntary* muscles, that is, muscles over which there is no control, begin to contract and relax. After this moment, which I call the point-of-no-return, ejaculation and orgasm are inevitable. Nothing the man can do can prevent it.

The contractions of the muscles suddenly become very strong. The first of these contractions forces the seminal and prostatic fluids with their load of sperms into the urethra. The second forces the semen up the length of the penis and a third forces the semen in the penis-urethra out of the opening in a strong spurt, which can be so strong that the semen is propelled anything up to two feet. Between five and eight of these contractions are required to expel most of the semen out of the penis. Not all the semen is expelled, however, and what is left is very rapidly increased so long as the man remains sexually stimulated. This allows him to have a second ejaculation within about twenty minutes if he is restimulated to orgasm within that time, though the volume of the ejaculate will be a little less than that of the first.

Orgasm as the outcome of love-making is brought about by the stimulation of the orgasm-producing nerves by the corrugated-like walls of the woman's *vagina*. For this to happen, the erect penis is put into the vagina and moved backwards and forwards by thrusting movements of the man's pelvis and buttocks.

The vagina is the complement of the penis. On the analogy that the penis is a sword, the vagina is its sheath. In fact, *vagina* is the Latin word for sheath. In a relaxed state the average vagina is about three-and-a-half inches long from the entrance, which is between the woman's legs – in the same position on her body that the man's penis is on his – to the back wall, where the neck of the womb enters it. It has, however, tremendous stretching qualities and can expand lengthways and sideways to accommodate any size of penis up to seven-and-a-half inches long or six inches in circumference without causing the woman any discomfort. Its inner lining, which is in a series of tiny folds which give it its corrugated-like effect, is of the same kind of special membrane that covers the penis-head.

At the entrance to the vagina are two sets of folds of flesh known as the *lips*. The cover of the inner, or lesser, lips, which form the entrance proper of the vagina, is of the special membrane also. Above the inner lips is a body ridge – which I call the *vaginal ridge* – padded with flesh and covered with the special membrane. About an inch above the vaginal opening and situated in the ridge, is the opening of the urethra. Above the urethra, at the apex of the ridge, is a tiny organ known as the *clitoris*. The clitoris, in fact, is a miniature penis, except that it has no opening. All of it, except the head, is embedded in the flesh of the vaginal ridge; the head itself is protected by a hood of membrane, as the penis-head in the uncircumcised man is covered by the head of the foreskin.

The inner lips and the whole of the vaginal ridge, including the urethral opening and the clitoris, are covered by the second fold of skin called the outer, or large lips.

The womb, in which the baby develops, and whose neck or cervix protrudes into the back part of the vagina, is a pear-shaped organ. About three inches long, two inches broad and about half an inch thick, it is mainly composed of muscles, and like the vagina, has tremendous powers of expansion which are essential for it to accommodate the growing baby. At the top end of the womb, on either side, are the *ovaries*, or egg-factories, which are joined to the womb by the Fallopian tubes.

These are all the primary sex-organs of the woman, more numerous, as one can see, than the primary sex-organs of the man – penis, testicles, seminal vesicles and prostate. The woman, however, besides being so well equipped with primary organs, also has secondary sex-organs which a man does not have, namely her breasts, which are connected to her sexual nervous system.

Like the man, the woman is sexually roused either physically or psychologically. Psychologically she does not respond so easily as the man. She is not sexually roused, as a rule, by the sight or the picture of a naked man, though many admit to being so roused by the sight of their fiancés or husbands naked, especially if the penis is erect. Some women, but not all, are stimulated by reading erotic descriptions – to which the great majority of men readily respond – and to erotic atmospheres. But taken by and large, the woman is nothing like so responsive to psychological stimulation as men are.

Physical stimulation of the vaginal entrance, the clitoris and the breasts, particularly the nipples, is far more successful in arousing women than any kind of psychological stimulation. Stimulation of the nipples by rubbing them gently between finger and thumb, or between the lips, or by sucking, not only causes them to fill with blood, stiffen and become erect like the man's penis, but to communicate rousing sensations to the clitoris and outer and inner lips. The clitoris undergoes erection exactly like the penis, while the inner and outer lips swell and open.

If direct stimulation is applied to the erect clitoris by the finger either of the woman herself, or of her partner, or her partner's lips and tongue, after a time the sensations begin to mount, and like the man she reaches a point-of-no-return, the inevitable conclusion of which is coming off. At coming off, the muscles of the womb and in the vaginal area contract and relax, like the man's orgasm-producing muscles, and are accompanied by indescribable sensations, just like the man's, which though concentrated in the clitoral and vaginal areas, flush throughout her body.

Besides these major sensitive zones – nipples, clitoris, vaginal lips and entrance – the woman has a number of other sensitive zones. Some of these correspond to the man's – the lips, behind the ears, the throat, the navel and the inner thighs and buttocks, all of which respond to the partner's caresses with lips, tongue and hands. In addition, she has the backs of her knees, her shoulders, her armpits and her belly. These, too, respond to similar attentions such as are administered to the others.

When both partners are sexually roused, sets of glands produce transparent slippery fluids whose sole object is to lubricate the man's penis and the woman's vaginal ridge, vaginal entrance and vaginal interior. In the man, these glands, known by the name of their discoverer as Cowper's glands, are inside the urethra at the base of the penis which is inside the body. The fluid they produce flows up the urethra and spreads over the penis-head. In the woman are two sets of glands, Skene's, which are situated in the vaginal ridge below the clitoris, and Bartholin's, which are in the vaginal entrance. In some men and women these lubricating glands produce so much fluid that in men it is sometimes mistaken for seminal fluid, and in women can be seen trickling over the vaginal ridge. In others, the amount produced is so little that it only just lubricates the penis-head and vaginal ridge and entrance; while some produce none at all, or so late – a second or two before orgasm – that one is not aware of it. Whether there is a copious flow or not, it has no important significance. A permanent source of good lubricating liquid is available in saliva, transferred from mouth to penis or vaginal ridge and entrance by the fingers.

I have already referred to the difference in time required by the male and female to reach orgasm by direct stimulation. The man needs between two and five minutes of such stimulation either with the finger, partner's mouth or her vagina to bring him off. The average woman, on the other hand, needs ten to fifteen minutes, and often longer, of direct stimulation of the clitoris or clitoral area to bring her off.

In addition to this, there is another important difference. My subject who put his penis into his wife's vagina as soon as he was roused and stimulated it by moving it back and forth until he came could not fail to bring himself off by these simple means. His wife, on the other hand, had never come off in all her twenty-two years of marriage because her husband's penis did not come into contact with her clitoris and so could not stimulate it to bring her to orgasm.

Among sexologists there is something of a controversy about what is called clitoral orgasm *versus* vaginal orgasm. Briefly it is that one side – and I am happy to say, the larger side – maintains that a woman can come off only as the result of clitoral stimulation, whereas the other side maintains that the stimulation of the interior of the vagina alone will bring her off if it is continued long enough.

Unfortunately some of the clitoral-orgasm school maintain that when the penis is put into the vagina, the upper side of the base comes into contact with the clitoris and the thrusting movements stimulate the clitoris and bring the woman off. In actual fact, to make such contact with the penis, the clitoris must be either abnormally large or long or very close to the vaginal entrance; *and very, very few women are so equipped*! But even if the penis did stimulate the clitoris the man would have to keep up his thrusting movements for about fifteen minutes, and there are very few men, even those who have trained themselves to retard their orgasms psychologically, who can stimulate the penis for so long without coming off.

The vaginal-orgasm school have recently received something of a set-back by the findings of two eminent American researchers into human sexual responses, Dr William Masters and Mrs Virginia Johnson, who have scientifically observed, with the help of the most sophisticated instruments, copulating couples under laboratory conditions. Masters and Johnson have discovered that the physical reactions of the various organs are exactly the same for every single orgasm the woman has, whether her clitoris has been stimulated directly or not. This seems to dispose of the main argument of the vaginal-orgasm school who accept the view of Freud (who first started the controversy) that the vaginal-orgasm was superior to the clitoral-orgasm, because it signified psychosexual maturity. But a far more important discovery was made by Masters and Johnson. They found that a woman bringing herself to orgasm by stimulating her vagina only with a substitute penis, nevertheless by the action of the substitute penis in the vagina, applied what might be called remote stimulation to the clitoris. This they found to be true when the penis itself was used to apply vaginal stimulation alone, and this led them to the discovery that the stimulation of the area immediately surrounding the clitoris takes place in the more customary positions for intercourse by the man's movements of his penis in the vagina. In other words, that there is no such thing as just vaginal stimulation alone by the penis.

One might think that, this being the case, my subject whose idea of making love was merely to put his penis into his wife's vagina and bring himself off would eventually bring off his wife. *Eventually* is the operative word here. He might do so if he could keep up quite vigorous movements of his penis inside the vagina for at least half an hour without coming off himself. Very few men, as I have remarked before, have this considerable degree of control. The most skilled would have to pause frequently and lie quite still in order that the orgasm-sensations might subside before they continued their movements.

These pauses, however, wreck the whole operation if the object is to bring the woman off as well. Once the stimulation of the woman has begun, it must be continued rhythmically and without pausing, except once very briefly, for in seconds her sensations can disappear altogether and she goes right back to the beginning.

To make up for the difference in pace, therefore, the man must stimulate the woman until she comes up to the point of no return *before he puts his penis into her*. This stimulation is known as *fore-play* or *love-play*. Both partners should take part in it, for the man, though actually not in need of stimulation, can still benefit from it considerably, since if skilfully applied it can intensify greatly the sensations he experiences at coming off.

Fore-play is a technique which needs careful study. The expert is not merely the man who can bring his wife off, but who can make each orgasm a memorable experience. If this may sound daunting, be reassured; there isn't a man who, given a hint or two of what is required of him, cannot acquire the technique provided he is prepared to take it seriously, and to experiment, using his imagination and the guidance of his partner. A good sex-manual will be of considerable help here, and beyond saying that a knowledge of the sensitive zones and the acceptance of the use of mouth and penis as stimulating agents as well as the hands are the basic requirements of satisfactory love-play, I would prefer to leave it at that. Get your book!

The object of fore-play, as I have said, is to lessen the time-gap between the male and female's need of stimulation to bring them to orgasm. Fore-play is continued until the woman judges that she will come if her partner puts his penis into her and moves it vigorously for a few seconds. There is a second difference between the man's and the woman's reaction to orgasm. Immediately after the man has come the tip of his penis is extremely sensitive and remains so for some minutes. Even if he could sustain his erection long enough after he has come to make the movements with his penis in the vagina which will eventually bring his partner off, this extreme sensitivity of the penis-tip after ejaculation would make it too uncomfortable for him to do so. The woman, on the other hand, experiences no such post-orgasm sensitivity in the vagina and, in fact, finds the movements of the penis within her after she has come off quite pleasurable. Some women – more than is realised – find their partner's attempts to bring himself off, having brought her off once, so exciting that they have a second, or, if the partner can delay his own orgasm for five minutes or so, a third orgasm before he reaches his climax. The lover who can draw such a response from his partner can be well pleased with himself; but even so, he should never rest on his laurels.

The technique of fore-play should be a continuing study. Boredom is one of the great, if not the greatest, enemy of sexual happiness. Many a man has steered his marriage on to the rocks despite the fact that he understood the need for fore-play, had studied the technique, had discovered the caresses which most stimulated his wife and invariably brought her off. The trouble was that having worked out a satisfactory routine of caresses, he was too lazy to experiment with others and used the same caresses in the same order every time he made love. As a consequence, the element of surprise, which plays a very large part in producing a heightened effect of stimulation, did not exist.

Margaret was a young wife of thirty who came to me once with just this problem. 'I shall go stark raving mad,' she declared extravagantly, though she really did feel she would, 'if Jack doesn't change his tune. I suppose I oughtn't to complain, really, because he sees to it that I come off every time, and that I am well satisfied, but, honestly, Robert, I'm beginning to dread the moment when he begins to caress me.'

'Tell me exactly what he does,' I told her.

'Well, first of all, he rubs the side of my throat with his thumb, then he leans over me, and after kissing each eyelid, he kisses my mouth and we spend some minutes deep kissing. As we are doing that he puts his hand on my right breast and strokes the nipple with the palm of his hand. After a few minutes of that, he begins to suck my left nipple, at the same time putting his knee between my legs and rubbing it against my pubic bone, while he takes my right nipple between his finger and thumb and rubs it with them. When he has done this for just so long, he takes his hand from my right breast and strokes my tummy for a bit – still continuing to suck my left nipple – and gradually slips it down lower until he is stimulating my clitoris and vaginal entrance with his finger. It takes him exactly six strokes of my tummy to reach my clitoris. He knows exactly how long to stimulate my clitoris before I am ready for him to go into me. Then he climbs on me. He stimulates my left nipple between his finger and thumb. He makes eight long slow thrusts, pressing hard against my pubic bone at the end of each, and then begins quicker thrusts, while he nibbles at the lobe of my left ear with his teeth. Within a minute, I should think, of this, I come. Ten or twelve more quick thrusts, and he comes.

'As I say, I never fail to come, and it's always good. At least it was, but recently once or twice I haven't come at all, though I've pretended I have. You may think I'm making this up, but I swear to you I'm not. I'm not only sure I'll scream one of these times – and soon – but I'm really afraid that unless something happens to make him change his routine even a little, I shall get a complex and not be able to come at all.'

'Why don't you tell him what you feel about it?' I asked.

'I couldn't. It would hurt his pride too much. He's really quite proud of the fact that he brings me off every time.'

I agreed that she might wreck their relationship if she did say anything to Jack, knowing him. On the other hand, he was on the point of wrecking it himself.

'There's only one thing for it,' I told her. 'You must break the routine yourself.'

'How?'

'Make love to him. Make him lie still, and you be the active partner for a change and finish with you astride him, telling him how to stimulate you with his hands, perhaps one at a breast and the other on your clitoris. Be quite firm about it, if he protests, though somehow I don't think he will. Probably he would like to change the routine but is afraid to, in case he doesn't bring you off by another set of caresses. It is laziness, certainly, but there may be this fear. I shall be very surprised if you don't come quite intensely, but even if you don't, pretend you have. Once you've broken the ice, insist on other experiments.'

It worked. But if Margaret had not plucked up courage and spoken to me about it, their marriage could have foundered on this one thing. I am not for a moment suggesting that they would have got as far as divorce; but I am quite sure that by the time they had reached their fifties, they would have become an embittered couple in every compartment of their marriage relationship, not only the sexual.

Variety, which can only be introduced into one's sexual life by a bold, adventurous spirit of experimentation on the part of both partners, is absolutely essential to avert boredom. This does not mean experimenting in the first three or four years of marriage, but a continuous search for new caresses, new positions, new aids to love-making, new thrills from the altar past the pension book. Unfortunately, far too many couples of my generation – those for whom I am particularly writing this book – have never had this urge for sexual adventure, or, if they have, have smothered it because they have not understood that sex should not only be a satisfying experience, but a frank, happy and psychologically gratifying experience, which it can become only if the lovers are never content with what they have. Sex is one of the few important things in life which flourishes on being given no rest; no rest, that is, from the determination of the lovers to make it even more perfect than perfection itself. This means a constant exploration on the part of both, and yet this aspect of sex is probably the most neglected.

Take, for example, the positions for coupling. In my study of the questionnaires which I sent out to couples of fifty and over, I have been amazed to discover the number who have used one (the face-to-face-man-above) or at most two (the face-to-face-woman-above) all their married lives. I asked them to say whether they had used any of the five most common positions, and left a space to describe any position they used with fair frequency outside these five. Those whose sex-life had, in their own admission, come to grief invariably left all six questions blank. But even if they had used the five positions they would have brought variety into their love-making, which would have kept their boredom from becoming complete. Consider for a moment the scope there is for variation in just this one phase of love-making. In *Sex Manners for Men* I have described thirty-two positions (or variations) for coupling; *I could have described another forty more*. Some of these forty would admittedly be outside the physical scope of the middle-aged, but the number they could still adopt would be a score, at least.

However, there is one good thing about sex. It is never too

late to learn, never too late to put things right. If you don't know fully the facts I have stated briefly in this chapter, a good first step, as I have suggested, would be to study them in more detail in a good sex-manual.

3: On Passing into Middle-age Sexually

As I remarked earlier from the moment when full physical maturity is reached – somewhere between twenty-five and thirty – a gradual degeneration sets in in all the physical organs of the body, including the sexual organs. The process of deterioration is so slow, however, that we are not aware of it until suddenly, as I have suggested, something happens to bring it home to us.

The rate of deterioration is variable from individual to individual and may be complicated by the effects of disease, which nearly always leads to a temporary and sometimes a permanent acceleration of the process. Thus, a fairly healthy man may be overtaken by old-age at sixty, whereas another man in the same state of general health may be alert mentally and spry physically at eighty; one woman may be lined in features and dowdy in appearance and mind at fifty-five, another may be physically attractive and a lively companion at seventy-five. On the other hand, there are men and women who, by reason of early ill-health or mental stress, may exhibit, and indeed possess, all the symptoms of old-age in their early and middle forties.

As a general rule, however, and for all practical purposes, fifty is the age at which, these days, the majority of men and women enter the middle phase of their lives. It is in the years immediately following fifty that awareness of the degree of encroachment that physical deterioration has made catches up with us. However, when I write such phrases as 'at fifty' or 'after fifty' I do not mean actually in the fiftieth year and before sixty. I am taking the decade merely as a peg which will give us a means of orientating ourselves *vis-à-vis* our middle-aged sexuality.

Men and women do not have the same experience of ageing sexually. For the woman there is the definite indication of the menopause or 'change of life'. During a period of from three to five years, the woman's ability to conceive and bear a child is slowly extinguished. The reproductive glands gradually decrease their productivity. The ovaries no longer produce a mature egg at the end of the woman's cycle as regularly as they did. With this irregularity of egg-production the natural accompaniment of the shedding of the egg during menstruation is affected. Between the shedding of one egg and the release of the next mature egg by the ovary, certain glands have been preparing the womb to receive the egg should it become fertilised by a sperm. The process of maturation is clearly closely allied to the process of relining the womb, for if a mature egg is not released by the ovary menstruation does not take place, since there is no lining to be got rid of.

Some women experience great irregularities in the cycle itself. There may be as long as six months or more between one menstruation and the next. and just as she is beginning to take hope that the menopause has been completed, she has a series of periods with only a few days between the end of one and the beginning of the next. For other women, this is a regular experience for two or three years. Yet others may go on longer than five years, during which they may have only half-a-dozen periods a year before the changes have become finally completed.

Nor are these irregularities the only disturbances with which many women have to contend. At times the woman may experience alternative waves of heat and cold – the so-called 'hot flushes' – followed by troublesome sweating. Few women escape this really uncomfortable symptom, though, as I shall describe later, the doctors can do much to alleviate the most unpleasant physical reactions of the body to the subtle changes taking place inside it. Many women, too, suffer from severe heart-pounding and headaches, and fits of mental depression and restlessness. They become very irritable, easily exhausted physically, feel weak all the time and unable to overcome the very noticeable slowing down of actions and reactions. Probably most upsetting of all for the woman herself is that in addition to these what one might call private trials, she finds that she suddenly begins to accumulate fat at an alarming rate, and in such quantities that she cannot disguise it, which brings her experience out of the private into the public sector of life, since all about her become as aware of this change as she is of all the others. She may be able to conceal the irregularities in her periods – except from her husband; she may retreat to the privacy of her bedroom at the onset of a hot flush; but her plumpness she cannot hide, even from the milkman. In these days of figure-consciousness, this increase in weight adds considerably to her pyschological worries.

The changes that are taking place within the body at this time are as subtle as they are formidable. There are in both men and women large numbers of glands, which are tiny organs that either secrete or excrete. They abstract certain chemical materials from the blood and change them into new substances which, in turn, stimulate and regulate various bodily functions such as growth metabolism (the process by which nutritive material fed to the body is built up into living matter or broken down into simpler substances), the excitation of internal organs to activity or the prevention of activity.

Glands may be classified into two main groups. If they secrete substances into a cavity or on to the surface of the body, such as the tear glands, the salivary glands and the sweat glands, they are called duct glands, or exocrine glands. If they secrete their chemical products into the blood or lymph, they are called ductless glands, or endocrine glands. The products secreted are called chalones and hormones.

Several of the ductless glands have a very important function in the development of sex and sexual activity. The hormones secreted by the thyroid gland, for example, affect sexual behaviour, for if the thyroid is overactive it increases the sex-drive; if underactive it decreases it. Another gland which also regulates the sex-drive is the pituitary gland, which is also known as the *master gland*, for its hormones stimulate or inhibit the functions of the other glands. If the pituitary does not function adequately the whole of the sexual apparatus functions inadequately.

The adrenals are another group of glands, located at the upper end of the kidneys. Their hormone is called adrenaline, which stimulates the activities of the heart and muscles and helps to maintain normal pressure in the arteries. If the adrenals are permanently overactive the individual will be overexcitable, ready for a fight and for violence at all times, and therefore hard to get along with. In many cases it has been found that over-functioning of the adrenals has resulted in an accentuation of the masculine characteristics and females become masculine in their behaviour as well as in their appearance. In other cases this overactivity of the adrenals has caused the development of the secondary sex characteristics – the swollen breasts of the woman, the deepening of the voice and the enlargement of the penis in the man, and the body hair of both sexes – at the age of seven or eight.

The group of glands which has the most direct effect on the sexual functioning of both men and women is the group known as the gonads. In the man the gonads are the testicles; in the woman they are the ovaries. Besides manufacturing sperms and eggs respectively, the testicles and ovaries produce a number of secretions, which between them are responsible for the development of the height weight, body fat, and the distribution of hair.

The testicles produce a hormone called testosterone, which is responsible for developing the maturity of the man's sex organs, and, from our point of view, but much more important, maintain his sexual desire. The woman has a similar hormone produced by the ovaries called theelin, which is believed to be responsible for the developnent of the womb, vagina and breasts, and which seems to influence her sexual desire.[1]

[1] Other glands which play an important part in the sexual experience of men and women are the man's Cowper's glands, which are situated at the base of the penis in the urethra, and which, when the man is sexually roused, produce a lubricating liquid that passes up the urethra and out of the opening where it spreads over the penis-head and makes it slippery. The woman's counterparts, the Bartholin's glands, situated in the entrance to the vagina, and the Skene's glands, sited just inside the urethra, both produce fluids which lubricate her vaginal-entrance and vaginal-ridge; and the man's prostate and seminal vesicles which produce secretions by which the sperms are carried from the seminal vesicles out of his body. *See also* p. 32.

The various hormones produced by the body and the effects they have on the bodily functions form an intricate and somewhat complicated subject which is difficult for the layman fully to comprehend. For our purposes there is no need for me to attempt to describe the full role which all play in the body's development and activities. On the other hand, it is useful for us to know that they all have very important roles, and that the sex hormones play a very prominent part in our sexual activities

Men and women produce both male hormones (androgens, as they are called) and female hormones (estrogens). When the androgens are predominant the individual is a man; when the estrogens are predominant, the individual is a woman. To give just one example of how each group of hormones affects the individual of the opposite sex, injections of the female estrogen have a retarding effect on cancer of the male prostate, while injections of the male testosterone relieve painful female menstruation.

The discovery of hormones was fairly recent. For some reason or other their study was neglected, and it was not until 1934 that the chemical formulas of the two most important androgens (male hormones) – androsterone and testosterone – were found. Even now, the effects of a number of known hormones are a matter of conjecture rather than proof. It is fairly widely accepted, however, that the sex hormones not only affect sexual functioning, but fashion sexual behaviour. The production of hormones varies from individual to individual, and it is thought that those with a high production of certain of the sex hormones are more sexually active – that is, subject to a stronger sex-drive – than those whose hormonal production is lower. To state it more concretely, the man whose sex-drive prompts him to make love to orgasm *daily*, or even more often, in order to obtain relief from sexual tension, produces more of the sex hormones, among them testosterone, which regulate the strength of his sex-drive, than the average man whose sex-drive prompts him to achieve three ejaculations a week to give him relief from sexual tension.

Now, the focal point of the menopause in women is the ovarian glands (the ovaries). To understand exactly what happens during the menopause, let me explain briefly the function of the ovaries.

The essential function of the ovaries is two-fold – to develop the ova (eggs) and to produce hormones. The ovum continues to develop after it has been fertilised by the male sperm and the ovary and its secretions play a major role in this development.

There are two ovaries, one lying on each side of the upper end of the womb. They are oval in shape like an almond and, like the man's testicles, feel solid. (The testicles and the ovaries are, in fact composed, of the same kind of tissue.) They are between one and one-and-a-half inches long and a quarter to half an inch thick.

Until the girl begins to menstruate, the surface of the ovary is smooth. As each egg matures, a small bump (known as a follicle) appears on the surface of the ovary, grows larger and larger, and at last bursts, releasing the fully ripe egg, which enters the Fallopian tube where it waits for a sperm to come along and fertilise it. If fertilisation does not take place it makes its way down into the womb, which at once begins to shed its lining. This lining makes its way out of the vagina – in menstruation – carrying the unfertilised egg with it. If, on the other hand, the egg is fertilised, it goes down to the womb and embeds itself in the lining.

Since all women produce far more eggs than they could produce children, by the age of forty-five to fifty the ovary becomes a mass of scar tissue, from the monthly rupture of the follicles, and eventually no more follicles develop. Only the tissue that secretes hormones is active, and the body adjusts itself to them by compensations of one kind or another, the chief being an increase in activity of the outer portions of the adrenal glands, which are capable of producing sex-stimulating hormones.

This last has a very high significance, and I shall return to it later. But I would like to underline it at this point, because what it means in practical terms is that though the ovaries may (and do) stop producing eggs and the ovarian production of sex-stimulating hormones markedly decreases, the woman's desire for sexual intercourse does not come to an end. Though not so pronounced, perhaps, so frequent, sexual tension does build up and can be relieved only by orgasm.

The changes which take place during the final years leading up to the menopause are subtle and gradual. Were it not for the symptoms I have already described the woman would probably remain ignorant of the hormonal changes.

However, as the years advance after the menopause has taken full effect, the gradual slowing down of the production of sex-hormones by the compensating glands does begin to have other effects which do come to the notice of some women. Perhaps the most common of these effects is the thinning of the lining of the vagina. Before the menopause when the vagina is receiving considerable stimulation from the estrogen hormones, its walls are thick and corrugated. With the withdrawal of this stimulation, but again by a very gradual process over at least five years, and, more commonly, much longer, the walls become paper-thin. This means that they cannot protect the urethra and bladder from the friction of the thrusting penis in coupling, and so the activity becomes painful. The penis can also cause pain, unless the husband is fully aware of the circumstances and conducts this phase of love-making accordingly, through the shortening and narrowing of the vaginal barrel and the constriction of the opening. While the shortening and lengthwise capacity for stretching may mean that the vagina cannot accommodate the full length of even the average six- to six-and-a-half-inch penis, the narrowing very rarely is of such proportions as to refuse admission to penises with girths up to five to five-and-a-half inches. As for the constriction of the vagina entrance, the pain that this gives rise to is not so much from the constriction itself as from the lack of lubrication. It is the experience of most women, though there are numerous exceptions, that the Bartholin's and Skene's glands function less fully, or cease to function altogether, after the change. The attempts of a dry penis to enter a dry vagina entrance can be very painful indeed for the woman. Fortunately, as I shall be explaining later, there are ways of eliminating all these various pains.

I am myself doubtful whether the male undergoes anything that can be likened to the woman's menopause. Those who claim that they do have not produced very convincing evidence, and a good deal more research will need to be carried out before I and those who think like me will be converted.

The female menopause means the complete end of the woman's fertility, and it is an experience undergone by *every* woman. The post-change woman, however, is not only capable of sexual desire, sexual arousal and acceptance of the penis in the vagina, but eventual satisfying orgasm. So long as she remains in good general health, she can lead an active sex-life well into her seventies. In fact, as I shall be pointing out again later, many women develop a far more active and satisfying sex-life *after* the change than they ever had before. But however active they may be, they can never produce a child.

Now it is a fact that most men in their fifties begin to have a gradual decline in fertility. In other words, their semen does not contain sufficient sperm or sufficiently healthy sperm to ensure that every time they make love in conditions otherwise favourable for conception, they would impregnate their partners. Nevertheless, the number of men in their sixties and seventies who have become fathers is considerable. I heard the other day of the case of a man of ninety, married to a twenty-seven-year-old, who fathered a child. There is certainly no case on record of a woman of sixty, even, becoming pregnant.

But even if the man produces no sperms at all, his sexual desire and his sexual ability to have satisfying orgasms do not likewise disappear. The latter, however, is dependent upon his being able to have an erection.

This is the crucial point, where large numbers of men fail. Impotence, partial impotence, weak erections that do not allow the penis to enter the vagina, retarded ejaculation – that is, a very long period of stimulation of the penis required to bring the man off, if he can be brought off at all – and, strangely, a reversion to a condition of the ardent days of youth, namely, premature ejaculation; all these are the troubles that beset the middle-aged male, and are regarded as signs of the male 'change of life'.

Though it is true that certain hormonal changes take place between fifty and sixty, which affect the action of the prostate and testicles, most of these troubles have psychological rather than physical roots. True, there is a slowing-down in the frequency of desire, but if the man who made love four times a week in his peak years can, at fifty or sixty, make love satisfactorily both for himself and for his partner twice a week, it is foolish of him to become disturbed by what he believes to be the approaching end of all his sexual activity. But it is this psychological disturbance which, in fact, undermines his desire, his physical responses and his performance. The vast majority of cases of partial or complete impotence and of weak erections are mainly the result of the psychological effects of the fear of impotence. In other words, we have here a vicious circle in which fear of becoming impotent creates impotence.

Again and again I have expressed the need for good general health in middle- and old-age as a criterion for normal middle- and old-age sexual functioning. If the general health is impaired, the sexual health is bound to suffer too. This, in its turn, adds to the psychological effects. Let me try to illustrate what I mean by the case-history of John W.

John was fifty-seven. He had been married for thirty-one years, and though the marriage had not been wildly romantic, his relationship with his wife had been an average and a happy one. She was two years younger than he, and had had her menopause early, so that she was completely over it by fifty-one. She was also an intelligent woman, and had decided that because she could no longer bear children, she was not going to allow herself to be transformed into a frump in middle-age. She took great trouble with her appearance, had her hair done weekly, sometimes more often, consulted a beauty specialist and learned to make herself up to the best advantage, kept her figure slim and trim and, since the children had left home, engaged in outside interests to keep herself mentally alert.

When they had first married in their middle twenties, John and Mary had made love on an average of three or four times a week. John had understood the need for acquiring a technique of love-making, and though he had not developed an expertise that could be called outstanding, more often than not he had made it possible for Mary to have a satisfying orgasm. She had no complaints on that score, though, she later admitted to me, there had been times when she had wished for more exciting love-making, though not often.

After her menopause she gradually began to realise that she

was becoming more preoccupied with thoughts of sex than she had been at any time during her earlier life, and that as a consequence her sexual desire was also increasing. Bluntly, she was roused more often, wanted to make love more often, and also wanted a deeper sexual experience than she had had before.

John, on the other hand, by this time had fallen into the habit of making love to her only on Saturdays or Sundays, and then not always every week. She would have made love every other day if she had responded always to her sexual promptings, but she did not criticise John for his lack of ardour, accepting what his behaviour implied – that his greatly increased responsibilities at work made him too tired for love-making during the week.

However, this did not solve the problem of her increased desire, and after a time, having come across my book *Mainly For Wives*, in which I advocate that wives should take the initiative and the active role in love-making, should they feel like it, and their husbands show no signs of being similarly inclined, she made one or two tentative approaches. To her delight John responded, but on a couple of occasions rebuffed her gently, kindly, but firmly.

Her successes, however, encouraged her. Then, for the first time in her life, she had a strong desire to caress his penis orally. 'I didn't know that lovers did such things,' she said, 'until I read your book. I hesitated for a long time, but I wanted to make love so much one night, and the desire to do this to John was so strong, I couldn't stop myself.'

John was surprised, but made no objections. The incident, on the other hand, suddenly brought him to with a jolt. He realised that Mary had changed. For the first time for a long time, he really noticed how attractive she was, and as he thought, it struck him that she was much more sexually active than she had ever been.

His work was tiring as well as exacting. Often he had to bring a briefcase full of papers home with him, and by bedtime all he wanted to do was tumble in and sleep. That is what he had been doing, but now he was aware that he ought to pay more attention to the new Mary. But he could not readjust to her straight away, and, in fact, though he kept telling himself he really ought to do something about it, he never did.

Then another incident occurred. He went to bed very tired one night, and when Mary wanted to make love to him, he refused, turned over on his side and went to sleep. A little later he awoke, and became conscious that Mary was actively attending to her own needs.

'I was a minute or two trying to make out what was happening,' he said. 'I thought at first that she was probably dreaming. But as she began to come, she made little sobbing noises which she had only recently begun to make when she came, and I realised that she was masturbating. I realised, too, that she would not like me to know what she was doing, so I pretended to be still asleep. I must say, though, that it upset me to know that she had had to help herself just because I had said no when she had begun to make love to me earlier.'

As a result of this incident he was shaken out of his rut. He really would do something about it. But almost immediately the increase in Mary's desire for love-making struck him even more forcibly than before, and in a moment of panic he thought, 'What if I can't keep pace with her?'

Instead of telling himself that of course he could he let the idea begin to nag at him. He ought to have made love to her at the first available opportunity. but he waited a couple of days, hoping she might make the first sign When she did not, he did make love to her. He had some difficulty in getting a really firm erection, however, and this added to his anxiety. The love-making from his point of view was a failure, because, for the first time in thirty years, he came as she touched his penis to guide it into her.

This was a fatal experience. Almost every time, for the next several months, that they made love, he either prematurely ejaculated or could not get a firm enough erection to go into her. He could not respond even to her oral caresses.

For a time both were plunged in despair, which did not help John at all, and it was in utter desperation that he went to see his doctor. Unfortunately, his doctor seemed more embarrassed than John was at having to tell the story 'of my failure'.

'It's nothing to worry about,' the doctor said. 'I'm sure it's just a passing phase. You've probably been overdoing it at the office. And after all, you know, you're not getting any younger. You can't expect to be as sexually active as a young man. I'll give you a bottle of tonic.'

John took the bottle of tonic faithfully, and though he admitted he felt less tired than he had for some time, it made no difference to his potency. Another month or two had gone by when he came to see me to ask me if I could recommend a specialist he might consult.

'I don't mind betting you've nothing organically wrong with you,' I told him, when he had related his story. 'Do you still have morning erections?'

He seemed surprised by my question.

'Well,' he said, 'come to think of it, I do. Not so often, perhaps, but two or three times a week.'

'In that case,' I replied, 'I think a psychiatrist would be able to help you more.'

'You mean you think I'm imagining I'm impotent?' he asked.

'Yes,' I said. 'If your impotence had any physical cause, that would prevent you having even an involuntary erection.'

'Can you tell me more?'

I told him what I thought had happened, as I have recounted in the story above. He said he would like to think over what I had said before taking professional psychiatric advice.

'All right,' I said. 'It's up to you, but don't waste any more time than you need.'

'You really think I can keep up with Mary?'

'I have no doubt about it. The trouble with you is that you've let your life be dominated by your work. Admittedly, you must be very tired some days, but you've got into the habit of going home tired, whether you are or not. In any case, the idea that a man can't make love when he's tired is very largely myth. You would have to be very tired indeed for that. Certainly, it can happen occasionally. But why not be content to let Mary take the initiative whenever she feels like it, if not staying the active partner right through, at least until she wants you to go into her?'

And I said more, to which I shall be referring later.

As it turned out, there was no need for him to consult a psychiatrist. He was able to readjust, on the basis of what I told him.

The case is by no means an uncommon one. More often than

not, the psychiatrist rather than the physician has the cure for middle-aged sexual disorders; and almost as often the man can cure himself if he will be patient and have a good honest chat with himself.

In cases where impotent, weak erections or retarded or premature ejaculation have causes that have no traceable psychiatric origin, there is also a definite absence of sexual desire. This stems from the fact that the androgen output of the testicles and prostate which control sexual desire has greatly depreciated or ceased altogether. This lack of hormone production can be corrected by injections of synthetic hormone of the right type. So there is really no need – except in a very small percentage of cases which will respond neither to hormone nor to psychiatric treatment – for a man or a woman to consider themselves incapable of sex in their later decades.

To sum up, both the man and the woman do undergo physical changes, the woman on a much greater scale than the man. But whatever the changes, whether it be the complete menopause of the woman, or the much less drastic glandular changes in the man, the sexual apparatus of both is normally quite capable of performing, though perhaps on a slightly reduced scale, as satisfactorily as it did in the past. Where there are detectable deficiencies – thinning of the lining of the vagina, failure or partial failure of lubrication, hormone under-production, and so forth – there now means on hand for correcting them.

The best way of avoiding sexual failure of almost any kind is to maintain regular love-making throughout life. I have already referred to the fact that the American researchers, Dr Masters and Mrs Johnson, have found that the more often a couple make love in the years twenty to forty the longer they will remain sexually active in the middle and later years. Though admittedly it is a bit too late to ensure prolonged love-making by trying to make up for lost time when middle-age has already arrived, nevertheless, regular and fairly frequent love-making – sometimes even when you are not prompted by desire – plus a new adventurousness in techniques, is one of the surest insurances for maintaining a satisfactory sex-life for most, if not all, of the rest of one's days.

4 : Do You Still Want To Have Sex Or Not?

Upon your answer to this question will depend whether you will actually have sex or not as you grow older.

As the story of John and Mary demonstrates, a great deal of the cause of sexual failure has its roots in the mind. There is absolutely no doubt that far too many men and women use the changes I have described in the last chapter as an excuse for ceasing to be sexually active. They seize on the pretext of feeling out of sorts, of hot flushes or headaches, of increasing plumpness of tiredness, of business responsibilities, of public work – in fact, the slightest, flimsiest reasons for rejecting any sexual approach that may be made to them or for refusing to make any response that is expected of them.

What they are really admitting is that they are so bored with sex that it no longer has any attraction for them. Or rather I should say, they are so bored with sex with their partner that it has no attraction for them any more.

Correspondent R is sixty-seven, his wife fifty-nine. They have been married for twenty-seven years and have two children, one of whom, a daughter, lives at home. He is a retired schoolmaster, but his wife is still teaching. They do not entertain very much: 'Perhaps once a month an old friend will call.' They hardly ever go out together: 'We have nothing in common, though in earlier days we had much.'

R is an amateur musician, playing three instruments and holding two diplomas. Mrs R's hobby is visiting stately homes, which she can only do occasionally. He does not accompany her, as he has arthritis in both ankles, and finds walking for long difficult.

At twelve stone, R is not overweight for his height (five feet ten inches) and age. Mrs R, who is five feet nine inches, and weighs ten stone, is trim and neat. She has good health, neither smokes nor drinks, nor takes pep-pills. R takes 'pills prescribed by my doctor to relieve the pain in my ankles'.

They married during the war, and at first their love-making was irregular for lack of opportunity. Neither, however, had a high sex-drive and when they were together after the war they did not make love more often than once in four days.

They share a double bed, but never have intercourse now, though R would like to very much, at least once a week. 'My wife is one hundred per cent frigid. She never proposes and never accepts sex.'

R does not have morning erections; he says he never has had; but he does still have strong erections, he claims, of the involuntary type; that is, he can induce an erection without direct stimulation of the penis. (*At sixty-seven, this is quite an achievement.*)

Mrs R had an early menopause, beginning at forty and finishing by forty-five. She was even lower-sexed than her husband. In the earlier years of marriage their technique of love-making was little more than rudimentary. He would caress her clitoris, and suck and fondle her breasts. On two or three occasions he applied oral caresses to her genital area. Exept when he specifically asked her to, she never caressed his penis with her hand.

On two occasions in their twenty-seven years of marriage, they made love with the wife above; apart from that they always adopted the man-above position. They have never made love except at night, and never anywhere but in bed.

'She required stimulation of the clitoris for never less than half an hour to bring her to the point where penetration was more or less easy. Very often she would let me stimulate her for an hour before she asked me to go into her. I have never really known whether she came off or not. She never seemed to thrill, or breathe deeply, or tremble, or give any sign that she had come. I always had to ask her, and she always said yes, though I am certain that she often never came anywhere near it. Sometimes I would have very much liked her to take the active role from beginning to end, but I couldn't ask her to, because we could never discuss sex. In all our married life, not a single word about sex – except my asking her if she had come, or her telling me to go into her – has passed between us. I tried to show her once what I would like her to do, but she gave me such a look of contempt and turned her back on me that I never dared try again. She made me feel really dirty.'

The Rs have not made love for the last fifteen years. R says, 'My wife is completely frigid, and now makes no attempt to conceal her hatred of sex. The marriage is really nonexistent and a misery. It was tolerable until her change of life when she was about forty-four, but I would give anything for a divorce, even at my age. For myself, I feel the urge as much as I did thirty years ago, but have no chance at my age of getting relief elsewhere.'

This is by no means an uncommon case. In fact, I am tempted to say that it is a typical example of the kind I most deplore. The Rs, since the very first weeks of their marriage, have never taken their sex seriously as part of their lives, and an important part at that. Certainly they have not used it as a visible symbol of their love for one another. I say nothing of the low frequency of their coupling. R was well below the average, as demonstrated by his 'once-in-four-days' programme. Mrs R's sex-drive was probably even less high-powered. On the other hand they were not faced with the problem of a highly-sexed partner married to a low-sexed one. The low frequency of their intercourse has, therefore, no significance. So long as they were both satisfied by it, once in four days was all they needed.

But they could have made this infrequent love-making exciting by developing a varied technique of fore-play, and using a variety of positions – even six or seven gives quite a choice. It was clear by what both said that Mrs R's upbringing had inhibited her considerably with regard to sex. Apart from the natural modesty which is innate in all women, inhibitions produced by puritanical attitudes seem to afflict more women than men. However, by patience, kindness and gentleness, a determined husband can remove such barriers for the good of both. Mr R made no attempt to do so, I think possibly because his sex urge was satisfied by his probably not very intense orgasms.

The result of this laziness and lack of interest was nevertheless tragic. Long before the wife's menopause had overtaken both of them, they were bored by sex. She welcomed the change to free herself from something which she had probably always found distasteful, and he made no attempt to woo her all over again. Ironically, at sixty-seven his sex-urge is strong for one whose younger-years' frequency was only once every four days, and this has made him bitter so that he feels his marriage has become a mockery and would dearly like a divorce, though he realises that this would not solve his sex-problem at his age. All my correspondents were anonymous, but if I could have got in touch with R I would have advised him to find someone to have sex with him, even if it meant buying the services of some experienced call-girl from time to time. I don't think he would have had to do this. I am quite sure that if he made a determined effort he would find an understanding middle-aged woman to become his mistress, if not his wife. It would take a certain amount of courage, perhaps, to face the publicity of a divorce at sixty-seven, but it would be short-term publicity, quickly lived down.

In contrast, let us consider the Ys. Y is fifty-two, Mrs Y is fifty. They have been married for thirty years and have two children, one of whom, a student, lives at home in the holidays. Mr Y is personal attendant (valet) to an industrialist and Mrs Y manages a shop. At five feet eleven-and-a-half inches and weighing fourteen stone, he is over-weight, though not grossly so, and has acquired a bit of a belly. Mrs Y is five feet four inches and weighs nine stone four pounds, which is average for her age and height. She keeps a watch over her figure and appearance.

They play cards and dance and have occasional drinks at home, visit pubs and friends. Y's hobbies are watching Rugby football, gardening and swimming; Mrs Y's are flower-arrangement, knitting and dressmaking. Between them they smoke thirty cigarettes a day and have the occasional bottle of wine and gin. Both enjoy perfect health and take no drugs of any sort. Mrs Y has completed the menopause.

When they were younger they made love every day, and now (at fifty-two and fifty) they still make love every night when it is possible for Y to be off duty. Y is away from home quite a lot, however, and they are not often able to make love every consecutive night, but they make up for this deficiency during the week, by four or five sessions of love-making through to orgasm on Saturdays and Sundays. He has very strong erections which he is able to sustain for an hour and a half at least. Mrs Y has mastered the technique of multiple-orgasm and often comes seven, eight or nine times to his once. He has equally acquired perfect control over his progress to orgasm.

From the beginning they have been adventurous in their love-play. They use oral techniques of caressing widely; though, somewhat strangely, they seldom deep-kiss. They make use of between fifteen and twenty variations of positions, and make love in the sitting-room, in the bath, in the car, in the country – in fact, anywhere they happen to be and feel the urge, and are assured of privacy. 'We have found,' they say, 'that you just try to have intercourse when you feel like it, and not wait.' If anything, since Mrs Y completed her menopause they make love more frequently than they did in the five years or so before she began it. Their one regret is that they have not more time for love-making.

The Ys, as did several other of my sexually-happy over-fifty couples, signed their questionnaires, and as I was interested in Mrs Y's multiple-orgasm experience, which they had discovered for themselves – they had never heard of Masters and Johnson – I wrote asking if they would be prepared to answer some supplementary questions, to which they readily agreed. I wanted to know, particularly, Y's penile dimensions, and the position and dimensions of Mrs Y's clitoris. The penile dimensions were four-and-a-half inches flaccid, six inches erect, and five inches in circumference when erect; that is, of average length but slightly fatter than average. Mrs Y's clitoris was three-quarters of an inch above the vaginal-entrance and about the size of a small pea when fully erect; that is, average both in position and size.

When using the conventional face-to-face-man-above position, Y does not make thrusting movements, but circular ones, 'as my wife says this movement gives her more satisfaction'. The penis does not touch the clitoris directly, and by the fact that this circular movement inevitably stimulates the general clitoral area and induces a series of rapid orgasms in Mrs Y, the Ys support the claim of Masters and Johnson that stimulation of the general clitoral area is as effective as more direct stimulation of the clitoris. The application of this circular movement also explains why Y is able to sustain his coupling for never less than half an hour, and often as long as an hour, before he comes; firstly, because the circular movement is less tiring than the thrusting one, and secondly, the movement is much less stimulating to the penis than the backwards-and-forwards movement; Y is, therefore, helped to control his progress to orgasm, though it is clear that he long ago established a great degree of this kind of control. In other positions, direct penis-clitoris contact is not achieved except in rear-entry with the wife kneeling. If she supports herself on her hands, contact is not made, but if she bends right down, with her face on the pillows, there is direct contact, and she can achieve up to nine orgasms in a coupling lasting three-quarters of an hour.

The experience of the Ys, who are, it will be remembered, fifty-two and fifty respectively, shows up the dismal failure of the Rs. One can tell immediately one begins to read their letters that they are a happy couple, very much in love, who have complete faith and trust in one another, not only sexually, but in all the various compartments of living. There is no dissatisfaction, no bitterness, and, by Masters and Johnson's law of the greater activity in early years – they married when he was twenty-two and she twenty – the longer the activity can be maintained in later life, I would not mind betting that when the Ys are eighty or more, they will still be making love and enjoying it.

I could have quoted from a score of couples in the early fifties whose wives have completed the menopause, to give as much force to my arguments as the Ys' story does. Mind you, the Ys are, I think, a little out of the ordinary run of people. Both are highly-sexed and, therefore, well matched, but I have a suspicion that Mrs Y's sexual nervous system is rather more highly responsive to stimulation than the average, though her sexual physique is average.

A good example from the sixty to seventy age-group are the Bs. He is sixty-one and she is seventy. They have been married for thirty-four years, which means that Mrs B married fairly late in life, at thirty-six, to a husband of twenty-seven. This is quite a large gap, especially when the wife is the senior partner, and one could reasonably have expected a breakdown in sexual activity in later life. But let us see what has happened.

B, who is five feet seven inches and slightly over-weight at eleven stone seven pounds, is a retired engineer who is now teaching. Mrs B, who is five feet three inches and weighs ten stone four pounds, is a retired teacher. They have one son who lived at home until he married three years ago. Both describe their general health as quite good, but Mrs B takes methyl dopa for her blood pressure and an occasional sleeping pill. B takes no drugs of any kind. B smokes a pipe; Mrs B does not smoke; both have an occasional drink.

They entertain quite a lot – friends dropping in for meals and relatives to stay from time to time. B has three absorbing hobbies – painting in oils, photography, and technical study (Mrs B knits and embroiders) – in connection with which they go on outings. They go away for occasional weekends and sometimes visit London.

Mrs B explains, 'We have had a very happy married life. I'm sure it could have been happier if we had been on our own. I had a strict upbringing with sex repressed. My father, who was a widower, lived with us for the first nine years.' When the father died, the Bs' son was five years old, and as there was a postwar shortage of teachers, Mrs B returned to teaching. She was then forty-five. She taught for fifteen years, retiring at sixty. She was sixty-seven when the son married and they at last had the home to themselves.

However, despite Mrs B's upbringing with regard to sex, and the imposition of looking after an aged father, and despite the difference in their ages, they did develop a satisfying sex-life. They made love two or three times a week. He had some difficulty in asserting control over his approach to orgasm in the early years, but they rarely spent less than half an hour on their love-making. Mrs B always came off, and did so without difficulty, largely as a result of their fairly adventurous love-play, which included cunnilingus. They also used a variety of positions, including rear-entry with the wife kneeling. They usually made love at night, though they occasionally did so during the day, but always in the bedroom because of the presence of the father or son in the house. B would like her to caress his penis with her mouth. He has told her this, and while she has not refused, she has been disinclined to do so, and B would not insist. She cannot explain her feelings about this, but both think it stems from her early upbringing. She is not at all averse to fondling his penis with her hand and caressing him elsewhere.

Let me quote B. 'The age difference was seen by my relatives as being ill-advised, but I can honestly say that from that day to this the difference to me has simply not existed. This happy state of affairs is due in part to my wife having an unusually young-looking and blemish-free body which is highly attractive to me, and this, along with a warm and loving nature, has helped our sex life. Unfortunately, my wife had very little sex knowledge when we married, which was not surprising taking into account her background, which was a fairly common one in her young days. But it did make it difficult for me to introduce sex reading. Due to caring for my father-in-law and also the war, and our son living at home, it is only during the last three years that we have experienced the freedom which we should have had during the first few years of our married life, to become really adjusted. But far from complaining, I am enjoying all the more the closeness and intimate freedom which is putting new life into our love for one another.'

Mrs B explains this in a little more detail. 'While I was teaching, I was often over-tired. It is only since we have had the house completely to ourselves on my son's marriage three years ago that we have felt that complete freedom. Then, too, the attitude to sex has entirely altered and we have recently enjoyed the many enlightening books on this subject and from them gained much benefit.'

Here we have a couple for whom, in late middle-age, sex took on a new lease of life, deepening their love for one another in the process. You may say that they were two very intelligent people for whom such a resuscitation would not be difficult. But it is utterly surprising how unintelligent otherwise intelligent, even brilliant, people can be about sex. The Bs are now having intercourse with the same frequency that they had when they were first married (two or three times a week), and this despite some difficulty B has with erection failing after he has gone into his wife. (He has consulted doctors about this, and is under treatment.) But Mrs B – she is seventy, let me remind you – has orgasm every time they make love. She has never come off during actual coupling throughout their marriage. Either he has brought her off by mouth-genital caresses before he has gone into her, or by stimulating her clitoris with his finger after he has come. I have recently had a letter from him saying that his recent treatment has improved his erections and though the penis 'may sometimes not be as stiff as one would wish, it stays stiff while I am in her long enough for me to come off. At sixty-one this isn't too bad, I suppose; but in any case, I am quite happy because I can come whenever I feel like it. My wife is much relieved, too, because, although she still does not come while I am in her, she is happier that I can now come each time she does, whereas for a time I would bring her off without being able to come myself.' Mrs B 'feels the need for orgasm'; in other words, her sex-drive is still active under her husband's encouragement.

The story of the Bs shows, in a quietly dramatic way, what can be done if two people, not highly-sexed, set their minds to refurbishing their sex-lives in late middle-age. From their marriage they had been quietly interested in sex, and while not terribly adventurous in their love-making, had nevertheless acquired techniques which prevented it from becoming boring. In contrast to the highly-sexed Ys their sexual experience is quiet and unflamboyant. The Ys could not go wrong, because of their sexual natures and their sexual curiosity. The Bs could have gone wrong, but had frustrated boredom and when, for the first time in their married lives, they had their home to themselves, they found a new freedom in which their love became deeper and more intimate, and this they needed to demonstrate to one another in the physical act that they could visibly and tangibly do so.

Pre-middle-age boredom with sex is one of the two great enemies of a happy and satisfactory sex-life in middle-age and beyond. It does not matter into which sexual category an individual or a couple falls – highly-sexed, average and low-sexed – a satisfactory and satisfying sex-life can be achieved if love-making is approached intelligently. Conversely, the highly-sexed can become as inactive – though probably much more frustrated, unless they seek outlets outside the marriage relationship – as the low-sexed, purely through falling into a routine of love-making which reduces the whole process to boring, automatic titillation with the fingers and bucking of buttocks.

I am strongly of the opinion that the present younger generations who are able to participate in sex without inhibitions will not have the middle-age sexual problems that those born between 1910 and 1930 have and will have. (By the time those born from 1930 onwards reached adolescence, the new trends in sexual freedom were beginning to operate.) They may have sexual problems, but I do not believe that boredom will be one of them.

Women are, I believe, slightly more susceptible to sexual boredom than men, and for this reason. Whether a man takes care over his love-making or just goes bang-bang-bang with his buttocks, he cannot fail to come, and though the orgasm sensations may not be all that ecstatic, they are still an experience and provide a relief from tension. But for the vast majority of women, even those who come fairly easily, the achievement of orgasm takes time and a careful stimulating technique, and very often may not arrive at all. Though extremely pleasurable, sex for the woman is a far more calculated process than it is for the man; and unless the man has acquired a technique which produces for the woman really voluptuous sensations while working up to the point-of-no-return, which makes the whole incident a pleasantly memorable experience, one can well understand a woman getting bored with the whole business. Even if she loves her husband and wants to give him pleasure, she can very easily withdraw from sex herself; but, good though her intentions may be, one-sided sex is no true expression of love. Mrs M is a good example of what I mean.

Mrs M is sixty-five, and her husband seventy. They have been married for forty-four years and have three children. She has not worked outside the home; he is retired, after having spent thirty years with an insurance company and ten years in the Civil Service. They do not entertain much in winter, but as they live by the sea they have a succession of friends and relatives to stay throughout the summer. They go shopping together occasionally take infrequent walks and visits to the theatre and cinema together and go to see friends. M's hobbies are boating, scientific reading and making things for other people (including two grandchildren) etc etc;' Mrs M passes most of her leisure time dressmaking, in Women's Institute activities, and 'doing many things for the children and others'.

At five feet ten-and-a-half inches, M is not over-weight at twelve stone, nor is Mrs M at nine stone for her five feet two inches. Neither smokes, and they drink very little, chiefly because they don't like it. M suffers from chronic insomnia, but otherwise his general health is good. For his insomnia, he has been prescribed Mandrax and Serenid D (a relaxing agent).

Until shortly before Mrs M had her menopause, they made love three times a week. 'Now we make love three times a year, perhaps,' says Mr M, 'though I feel the urge at least weekly. I did not have any difficulty in learning to control my progress towards orgasm, because little control was necessary, as my wife preferred short intercourse – say, five to ten minutes. You see, she always has been and is much less intense than me.' (I think he means by this last sentence that Mrs M's responses are less intense, and that she was far more easily satisfied than he.)

Their technique of love-making was rudimentary; he would stimulate her clitoris with his fingers and suck her nipples and she would fondle his penis. They very, very rarely used any position but the face-to-face-man-above, and their one variation was woman-above, except that sometimes when they were young, they would couple standing up when out on country walks. (In view of the the eight-and-a-half inches difference in their heights, this standing intercourse could not have been very satisfactory to either.)

When they were younger they used to make love naked, 'but now my wife likes to keep something on. No, I don't have any trouble getting an erection, but my penis never gets as stiff now as it used to. I think it would get stiffer if she would kiss it or stroke it more, but apart from playing a minute or two with my penis, she does nothing. What I would like her to do most of all is to suck my penis. I asked her to once and she did, but she was so afraid I would come in her mouth, though I promised her I wouldn't, that she would do it only for a few seconds, and I never liked to ask her again. But sometimes I get such a craving for it that I just don't know what to do. If only she would be a little more demonstrative, but now she is more passive than ever. I have absolutely no idea whether she has ever had an orgasm or not. At the beginning I used to ask her if she had come, but she never really said. "Don't worry about me," she used to say. "If you're satisfied, I'm happy." I would often suggest making love at times during the day, but she always put it off. She has always considered it "a messy business", and her excuse for not having it during the day was that she would have to bathe afterwards. She always has bathed in the morning.'

The picture emerges of Mrs M having practically no interest in sexual activity herself, but being quite prepared to allow M to satisfy his urge with her – because she appreciated his need to do this – so long as he did not take too long about it. But it is her very acquiescence in an almost completely passive role that has frustrated M most. If she had fought him a little, or he had not been quite the gentleman that he obviously is, or had used his imagination and tried to win her to a more active participation in sex, he would have been far less complaining than he is now.

In fact, the root of his cause for complaint lies in himself; for she is still as acquiescent as ever she was, and would undoubtedly join him in intercourse more frequently if he showed he wanted it. The degree of her acquiescence is really quite remarkable. 'When we were young and out for walks together we often had intercourse standing up. Today she says that this would make her uncomfortable, so I find a suitable spot and masturbate, and she understands that I like her to watch. Sometimes, when she knows that I'm feeling a bit randy, she offers to help me masturbate. I say "help", because her hand quickly gets tired. I now find this as satisfying as intercourse, and that is why I don't insist that she lets me go into her.' (This resolution of his mild exhibitionist tendencies is probably what prevents him from becoming actively exhibitionist, and falling foul of the law. This exhibitionism is a not uncommon feature of elderly male sexual activity where the wife rejects all forms of love-making and intercourse.)

His own shortcomings he unconsciously reveals in his final

remarks. 'May I add that my wife seems fully to understand my sexual desires are stronger than hers. She hasn't answered your questions to wives, not because she would be embarrassed doing so, but because she has always had difficulty in expressing her thoughts. *I would like to mention that never, during our entire forty-four years of marriage, have we had any disagreement on sex matters.*' (The emphasis is his.)

They would be in a much happier situation today if they had.

Here, then, we have four types of cases, in only one of which are things as they should be sexwise. Lack of adventurousness in love-making quickly leads to boredom, and boredom with sex then introduces all kinds of psychological factors which eventually bring about marital disharmony. I have been taken to task on occasions because in *Mainly for Wives* and *Sex Manners For Men* I have concentrated on the techniques of physical sex, with only passing mention of the emotional and psychological aspects of sex. I have done so quite deliberately, for, while I recognise that there are cases in which any sexual trouble there is may be initiated psychologically or emotionally, I am firmly convinced that in the vast majority of cases sexual boredom induces emotional and psychological difficulties. In other words, where there is physical sexual harmony based on sexual frankness between the two partners, and a technique which provides a wide variety in love-making and coupling (the wider the better), there is far less likelihood of psychological and emotional difficulties arising. That is, look after the physical side of love-making and the psychological side will usually look after itself.

This certainly applies to sex between two people in the transition from the peak to the declining maturity of old-age. I have what I regard to be definite proof of this. Again and again, and again as I have studied the results of my survey, I have had it forcibly brought to my attention that where there has been a happy sexual relationship with a variety of activity, sexual activity has not only continued into middle-age and beyond, but has become an even more expanded experience; while, conversely, where sex has ceased to play a significant part in middle-age and post-middle-age, it has never played a significant part in pre-middle-age.

Women who have become bored with sex, seize thankfully on the menopause to remove it from their experience altogether. It has never meant much to them and they can easily get on without it and not have any sense of loss. If the urge should rear its ugly head very very occasionally, then, if it cannot be sublimated masturbation is far more preferable to intercourse. (At the back of this excuse is their comparative difficulty in reaching orgasm. If they had the same rapid progress as men, I believe these women would not exist.)

It is interesting to note that these women are the women who make no effort to control their middle-age spreads – brought about by hormonal changes – who seem to lose interest in their appearance, even to the extent of adopting dowdy clothes, and who, if asked, will reply that in their view sex is unbecoming in middle-aged and elderly women. These are chiefly unconscious tactics to ward off the sexual attentions of their mates by appearing physically unattractive.

(I hasten to make it clear that not all women with middle-age spreads are not interested in sex.)

Mind you, the faults are not all on the woman's side. The man aids and abets her, though he may protest that he would like sex, but his wife won't co-operate. More often than not, you will find that the partner of the woman I have described above is the man who lets himself go physically to seed after fifty. He develops a paunch, he smokes and drinks moderately heavily; all three of which physically affect his sexual responses.

However, the true counterpart of the middle-aged woman uninterested in sex is the man who makes his office responsibilities the excuse for discontinuing sexual activity, at any rate on the scale of the younger man. Admittedly, around middle-age most men are at a vital stage of their careers, especially if they have not yet reached the top, but are near it. They have only another fifteen years to go before retirement, and since so many pensions are based on the salary or wages a man was receiving in the last three or four years before he retired, the comfort of his old-age will largely depend on his getting as far as he can in the next fifteen years.

Office responsibilities are tiring, about that there is no doubt.

But it is not just the office which provides his worries. Because of the age at which the 'fifties generation' married - twenty-eight to thirty – the education of the children, feeding and clothing them are more expensive than they have ever been. Wages and salaries in these days of constantly rising taxation and cost of living have also a way of lagging behind needs. The early years of middle-age are, indeed, trying and worrying years, and are not made more bearable by the inevitable physical changes which overtake a man at this time.

As I have said earlier, some men panic when they become aware that they are slowing down physically, and indulge in some quite bizarre behaviour in order to prove to themselves that they are not so old as their bodies are constantly reminding them that they are. But far more withdraw from sex, if not completely, then almost so, using chiefly their physical tiredness as an excuse. What they do not appreciate is that a man has to be very tired indeed before he becomes sexually unresponsive. They are equally ignorant of the fact that love-making when they are tired, if it is taken gently, preferably with the wife the active partner, can be more relaxing than the deepest sleep. The relief that orgasm provides is not purely in the sexual system alone, but if it is thoroughly satisfying it dissolves other nervous tensions, too, and relaxes the mind wonderfully. Tiredness, in fact, is the least feasible excuse for avoiding a good session of love-making culminating in a satisfying climax. Afterwards sleep will be more refreshing, because the worries which the love-making has successfully pushed into the background remain there.

Ignorance of rather more sophisticated sex-knowledge is, unfortunately, a common failing in the present generation of over-fifties. This is not their fault. When they were younger, sex-manuals were not so readily available as they are now; sex was still far less openly discussed than it is now by our children, and, indeed, our knowledge of sexual functioning, though still very incomplete in some areas, was far less advanced. Nor have we taken the trouble to catch up. This has left us with some very rum ideas about sex.

I had this letter the other day from a woman.

Dear Mr Chartham,

My husband, who is fifty-four, has decided not to have intercourse any more. He says that he has read somewhere that ejaculation of semen places a greater and greater physical strain on a man after he has reached fifty, and that if he continues to have regular intercourse he will have a shorter expectation of life than if he shuns sex altogether.

Is there any truth in this? If not will you please do your best to convince him there is not. I hope there is not, because, although I am fifty, I still have quite a strong sex-urge, despite the fact that I have got over the menopause, and I would be very unhappy indeed if I thought I would have to go without sex for the rest of my life.

I have tried to tell him I am sure he must be wrong, but because I cannot produce medical evidence, he will not take any notice. I am sure that where I have failed you could succeed.

There is no truth in the husband's idea at all. The belief that a man is physically weakened by loss of semen goes back many thousands of years, but it is based on an entirely false notion of the nature of semen as a secretion and of its composition. When I was twelve and being prepared for confirmation, I was warned by the priest against masturbation, not only on the grounds of sinfulness – 'Wasting one of God's most precious gifts' – but because of its potential to be physically harmful. 'Semen is produced from the blood,' the priest told me. 'If it is not used, it goes back into the bloodstream and enriches it. If it is lost in masturbation, the blood becomes poor in quality and the health of the whole body suffers as a result.'

That was in 1922. We know now that semen is what is termed an *external secretion*. Once produced by the testicles it can never find its way into the bloodstream.

Yet only the other day, I read this in an American book which was published as late as 1956: 'Since semen contains sex hormones, by conserving it, rather than wasting it in sexual indulgence, these valuable hormones are saved and reabsorbed into the circulation.' (This is virtually what my priest was saying thirty-four years earlier.) The author went on: 'It is said that an ounce of semen is equivalent to forty ounces of blood from which it is made. With every seminal discharge the body loses its most valuable chemical constituents, highly important for the nutrition of nerve and brain tissues. Woman also loses her vital substance with each sexual act. This explains the short lives of the wives of passionate men and prostitutes.'

Absolute poppycock, the whole lot of it!

The wives of passionate men do not have short lives, and most prostitutes die of venereal disease.

Semen is composed of three several constituents, each produced by a different set of glands. There are the sperms produced by the testicles, seminal fluid by the seminal vesicles and the ducts of the epididymis and vasa, and prostatic fluid manufactured by the prostate. Seminal fluid contains large quantities of simple sugar, while the prostatic fluid has high concentrations of citric acid, ascorbic acid (vitamin C) and other chemical substances, many of them enzymes. There is also bicarbonate present and phosphate. There are no sex hormones in it. All the ingredients, one of the largest of which is water, are drawn from the food supply in a never-ending process. Before semen is discharged either during intercourse, wet dreams or masturbation, it is stored in the seminal vesicles. When these reservoirs become full, because of the ceaseless production, they have to be emptied, and if this is not done by love-making or masturbation, it is done for one in a wet dream. But the storage operation itself has already put it out of circulation, and it is no longer a part of the body's economy.

As Dr Isadore Rubin has pointed out, 'If the theory that seminal discharges weaken the body and shorten life were true, one would expect to find that married men have a shorter life expectancy than bachelors, who have less opportunity for intercourse. Actually, the reverse is true – it is the married men who live longer.'

The argument, in fact, holds no water whatsoever, and if any of my readers have been using it as an excuse for avoiding sex, he had better be honest and admit that, truthfully, he is bored to death with sex and cannot be bothered with it any longer.

As I have said, more women than not seem to be able to withdraw altogether from active sex. This is not true of men. Even where a man is too lazy to adjust himself to his changing sexual requirements, and seeks refuge rather behind one excuse or another, there are times – unless he is totally impotent – when his sexuality will impinge on his consciousness in morning erections. The awareness of an erection, whether it is involuntarily or automatically induced, gives rise to sexual thoughts. Admittedly these may be fleeting, especially if the erection is not very strong, but they serve to remind the man that the fire that once burned in his loins has not completely gone out. If he has fixed it in his mind that his wife is to blame for the banishment of sex from their relationship, these are the times when he becomes bitter, and if these occasions occur frequently, he soon develops into a frustrated crabbed old man, aged before his time. Then he wishes he could get his sex elsewhere, and yet he is too lazy to do anything about it but complain, mostly to himself, thus adding to the volume of his bitterness, excusing his laziness by moaning, 'I don't know where I could get it at my age'. Or he may – and this could be very serious – he may turn his attention to small children. This danger, and others, are always present when an elderly man is deprived of an outlet for his sex, besides masturbation.

It would be unfair of me to give the impression that in relationships that develop like this one, the woman is always to blame. She may find that, with the release from the fear of pregnancy, her desire for sex has taken on qualities which it never had before, when it was inhibited by this very real fear. Suddenly she finds that she wants to make love with double the frequency that she did when she was in her mid-thirties and forties; and she finds, too, that love-making has become a vastly more pleasurable experience than she can ever remember it. If she is married to the lazy man, she can become as frustrated and bitter as any man. What upsets her, almost as much as being deprived of love-making itself, is her failure to rouse her man sexually. She takes great trouble with her figure and her appearance; she makes herself, by all the means she can summon, physically desirable. That was how she won her lover at the beginning, and she believes she should be able to win him this way now. And so she should! What actually happens is that it is brushed aside with weary rejection – 'I'm sorry, I'm too tired.'

Equally galling, in some cases, is the panic into which a sexually transformed wife may throw a husband, as a result of which he develops psychological impotence. Many women feel this kind of rejection even more than rejection through mere laziness. They regard their husband's impotence as the final insult, chiefly because there is nothing they can do about it. Such women do not accept this situation, even if it gets them nowhere. If anything, they trim their figures even more, dress even more smartly - and become more deadly bitter than any man.

I know one such couple. Before and during the menopause, she was over-plump and dressed accordingly. Then suddenly a transformation began, and was so striking that one could not help noticing it. In fact, one could watch it going on under one's eyes. But as time passed the sparkle went out of her eyes and her lips took on a grim, cynical line. You could see the discontent oozing out of her.

Before long they were bickering, not between themselves in private, but in public. They said the most unpleasant things to one another, at first making pointed veiled comments and later direct references to the other's sexual failings. (*He:* 'You're sex mad!' *She:* 'He can't even rise!') She was much more cruel than he, and if she had only had a faint glimmer of the psychology of sex, she would have realised that her treatment of him was designed not to restore his virility, but to destroy it completely, perhaps for ever.

They are still at it. One would have thought that after some years she would have lost heart, except that a 'woman scorned' is as powerfully true in this context as in any other. But instead of reverting to her pre-menopausal dowdiness, she keeps up a constant struggle with her figure, spends a small fortune on clothes – which, fortunately, she can afford – and has recently had her face lifted and cosmetic surgery performed on her breasts. Since local gossip is mum on the subject, one can accept as true, I think, that she has no lover. It is all a sad, sad tragedy. They would be happier divorced, though she is still in her middle fifties and he in his early sixties; but divorce is taboo in the middle-class milieu in which they exist.

While I have a good deal of sympathy for him, I have to admit that basically the fault lies with him. I do not believe he was so blind that he did not notice the physical transformation in her - she is a very attractive woman indeed - though he might have been thick-headed enough, at first, not to appreciate that the motivation of the transformation was sexual. But she obviously did not keep quiet about her needs when she found he was not responding to her physical allurements. At her first overt approach he should have pulled himself together, like John did in the case I have quoted earlier. But he was too lazy, though not too insensitive to be hurt; and the hurt has now made it impossible for him to do anything about it, except undergo intensive psychiatric care.

The only consolation I can personally find in all these cases is in my statistics, which show that happy, sexually satisfied over-fifty couples outnumber the drop-outs by two to one. But this is far too high a proportion of drop-outs in any case, so my consolation is small.

5 : If You Don't Want To Be A Drop-out, Read on!

If you are a drop-out already, this does not mean that you have to remain one, but you have to make up your mind yourself. All I can really do is to try to encourage you, by assuring you that it is never too late to rehabilitate your sex life, and that the ways and means of doing so are not difficult, though they do require a little patience and perseverance to be successful.

My I address myself to the men first?

First of all, I think you must adjust yourself to the slowing up of all your physical functions. You must accept that you simply cannot do all the things that you have been able to do in the past, because the machine with which you did them is getting a bit worn. On the other hand, good and sensible servicing will mean that you can slow down the wearing out process; and this is particularly true of the sexual apparatus.

I can understand the man who, in his young days, enjoyed his sex and made love four or five times a week, getting into a bit of a panic when he suddenly realises that, at fifty-five or so, he wants to make love only two or three times a week. *Wants* is the operative word here. He made love four or five times a week because his sex-drive made him *want* to. Now his reduced sex-drive makes him *want* to make love only two or three times a week, but, when he does make love two or three times, on each occasion his enjoyment of it and his satisfaction are no less than they were on each occasion when he made love more often. In other words, his two or three times give him the pleasurable relief from sexual tension which his slightly reduced sex-drive dictates.

I am sometimes asked why there should be a reduction of the sex-drive. The people who ask the question are, I think, confusing sex-drive with sex-behaviour. Sex-behaviour in the lower animals is instinctive. In man, the use of the instinctive impulse for the purpose of releasing tension and thus, for pleasure, is largely, if not entirely, learned. We have a control over our instincts, which allows us to forbid certain manners of sexual behaviour, while tolerating others or demanding yet others.

We have no control over our sex-drive, however, purely because, unlike our sex-behaviour, which is a faculty of the intellect, it is operated by certain chemical processes taking place within our bodies. The sex-drive is inborn, resulting from the interaction of various glands, such as the testicles (male gonads), the thyroid and the pituitary, the latter stimulating the production of the sex hormones. The psychological expression of sex-drive is sexual desire, that is, the desire to release the tension built up by the sex-drive.

This tension is produced by the secretions of the various glands, and also by the action of the sex hormones. I have a theory – which has not yet been attacked or shown to be wrong – that the major part of this tension is centred on the seminal vesicles. I believe that the secretion of the fluid produced by the vesicles, plus the build-up of the sperm in the vesicles - both of which are continuous processes - eventually fills the vesicles to bursting point. This over-fullness creates tension by pure pressure in the seminal vesicles which is experienced physically as a kind of edginess and is communicated to the erection centre. The release from this tension can be obtained only by emptying the seminal vesicles, which is done automatically in wet dreams or deliberately by love-making or masturbation.

One of the criticisms that might be levelled against my theory is: why should some men find that one ejaculation does not satisfy them and they feel the need for a second (and sometimes a third) within an hour or a couple of hours? Or why, when the average time for the build-up of tension is say, two days, should a man want to make love on consecutive days? I think I have the answer to these questions too, based on personal experience and on the experience of a small team of associates who co-operate with me when I have a need to explore various aspects of sexual behaviour.

The potential critics would be justified, on the basis of my theory, in asking why an ejaculation, no matter how much semen is expelled, does not apparently relieve the tension since the seminal vesicles are no longer full. My answer to this is that if the seminal vesicles have been over-distended for a period of twenty hours at least, it takes anything up to an hour, perhaps more, for them to resume their normal size. (By the way, the seminal vesicles are never completely emptied by one ejaculation, which is why semen is always emitted in all ejaculations even when they follow at close intervals of time.) Until the seminal vesicles have returned to their normal size, the sensation of tension continues to be felt, and prompts the man to seek further relief in orgasm.

Secondly, it may be asked why, when a man is apparently satisfied by a first-rate orgasm, if he seeks a second orgasm within, say, half-an-hour or an hour, as soon as he begins to make love to achieve this second orgasm, does the tension rapidly build up. My answer to this is that I believe that as soon as sexual stimulation begins the production of seminal fluid is greatly speeded up so that within ten minutes or a quarter of an hour, the seminal vesicles are filled and creating tension. If I am right about this, and I believe I may be, this would explain why a man who at, say, 6.5 pm has no sensation of tension at all, sees a beautiful woman at 6.6 pm, has an erection by 6.7 pm and experiences tension at 6.10 pm of such intensity that he must have an orgasm. It would also explain why a man who goes to bed at 10.30 pm without any conscious desire to make love, at 10.35 is sexually caressed by his wife, has an erection at 10.36 and experiences intense tension at 10.38 pm. In both examples, the seminal vesicles may be from half to three-quarters full – at 6.5 and 10.30 respectively – but the speed-up of the seminal fluid production, once stimulation, either cerebral or manual, has begun, fills the seminal vesicles in seconds, a process which would normally take several hours to complete.

Finally, if I were asked how I would account for it that if a man has to have two or three orgasms completely to relieve his tension, the volume of semen spurted in the first ejaculation is greater than at subsequent ejaculations, my answer would be as follows. As soon as the much swollen seminal vesicles are given the signal to expel their fluid, they call into play much stronger muscle-reactions than if they were producing just that degree of tension which makes a man conscious of sexual desire. Masters and Johnson have reported that *all* their study-subjects state that ejaculations subsequent to the first are accompanied by less intense orgasm-sensations than the first one. This is one small point on which I disagree with these two eminent researchers. From personal experience and from the experience of my collaborators I would say that the opposite is the case: that when the seminal vesicles are over-full the orgasm sensations are much less intense than when the seminal vesicles are 'comfortably' full. I believe more research is needed into the aspect of the male response experience.

I have lingered rather over this question of sexual desire being regulated by the fullness of the seminal vesicles because I believe it has a direct bearing on the drop in frequency of sexual desire as one gets older. Past fifty the glands begin to slow down the speed and quantity of the secretions they produce. It follows, therefore, that the seminal vesicles take longer to reach that state of repletion at which they provide a degree of tension which forces itself on the sexual awareness of a man. Whereas earlier they filled up to this extent every two or three days, now they fill up only every three or four days, and, as they slow down even more as he grows progressively older, so his desire becomes progressively less frequent. When he makes this discovery, therefore, there is no need for him to panic and, by imagining that he is on the verge of impotence, actually make himself impotent. The fact that he is making love less often does not automatically mean that his orgasms are going to be less satisfying.

As I never tire of saying, all sexual response and the reactions to it differ not only from individual to individual, but from time to time within the same individual, even when he is at the peak of his sexual capacity. This, as between individuals, is demonstrated in the three main categories into which we sexologists, purely for convenience sake, divide the sex-drive capacity of men and women: that is, highly-sexed (those who need relief from tension daily or more often), the average-sexed (those who need to make love three or four times a week), and the low-sexed (those who feel the need to make love only once a week, once a fortnight or even once a month). Because a man – or woman – is urged to make love once a day or two or three times a day, as some are, you must not think that their experience of orgasm is either more intense or more satisfying than those whose need for orgasm is only once a month. In fact, the highly-sexed do seem to experience much more intense orgasms than the low-sexed, simply because their orgasm-producing equipment is much more sensitive. But that is not the point. The point is that though they need one, two or three orgasms every twenty-four hours – which is the norm for them – their orgasms satisfy the demands of their particular sex-drive; while those who need only one orgasm a month – which is the norm for them – are equally satisfied with their monthly orgasm. While the highly-sexed *need* their highly intense orgasms, which make them involuntarily moan, cry, scratch and even momentarily pass out, the low-sexed have need of no such intense orgasms. They are perfectly satisfied with an orgasm whose intensity the highly-sexed would scarcely notice. *Satisfaction, personal reaction to personal sensations, is the criterion; not the intensity, nor the frequency, of the experience.* The middle-aged man who feels the need to make love less frequently than when he was younger has, therefore, no need to fear that he is becoming impotent. It is merely that his norm is changing slightly. So long as each orgasm is as intense as he and his partner can make it, and the result completely relieves his tension, he has nothing to fear and everything to gain by accepting the new frequency of his sex-drive.

The operation of the woman's sex-drive is not so mechanically operated as the man's. (Mind you, the man's sex-drive capacity does not rely entirely on his chemistry and hormonal production; psychological factors are also involved, though I believe the main-spring of his urge is physical. The woman has not, for example, any equivalent of the seminal vesicles, though her ovaries are an evolution of them; nor does she have an ability to ejaculate, for she produces nothing equivalent to semen. Her sex-drive is controlled by hormone production to a large extent.

I am beginning to gather data to try to discover whether women with a larger and more prominent clitoris than average have a more frequent sex-drive than those with an average or smaller clitoris. I have been put on the track of this possibility by two or three random observations that have come my way. If I do find a relationship of any kind, then it seems to me that this might lead to a more definite discovery of the role of hormones in controlling the female sex-drive. I might discover, for example, that the large clitoris is formed by the above-average production of the male sex hormone which is present in all women, just as some female sex hormone is present in all men. I would work on the basis that as the penis is developed at puberty, and thereafter until physical maturity is reached, by the speeding up of the production of the male sex hormone, so the size of the clitoris might be determined by the activity-rate of the male sex hormone component in women. As everyone knows, the clitoris started out in the foetus as the penis, and it was the dominance of the female sex hormone which arrested its growth at the rudimentary stage – as soon as the male X-chromosome, which determines that the baby shall be female, began to assert itself – and was also responsible for the eradication of the testicles and the formation of the womb and vagina.)

There is, however, still a tremendous amount of research to be done on the subject of the woman's sex-drive. The theory of hormonal production as a primary source of the female sex-drive derives support from the fact that the average woman experiences a rise in the frequency and intensity of her desire to make love during ovulation; that is, when the ripe egg is released from the ovaries. Many women also report that they have an upsurge of desire during menstruation, when a new wave of hormone production is taking place.

Nearly all researchers have remarked, however, that except in unusual cases the woman's sex-drive is not so frequent as the man's. This does not mean, of course, that the woman is less easily satisfied by her orgasms than the man. With her it is also the satisfaction provided by orgasm that must be the criterion, not the frequency of her orgasms.

It is will known that a woman does not have to be roused in order to take part in intercourse, whereas the man cannot do so without being roused, since his penis will not become erect unless he is. So long as the penis can be put into the vagina she can play her role in coupling. It is unlikely that she will have an orgasm if she remains unroused, though I have had it reported that one or two women come off although there has been no erection of the clitoris and swelling of the vaginal entrance and the outer and inner lips. (I very much doubt whether these women did *not* experience erection of the clitoris and swelling, but as I was in no position to observe them, I have to accept their assurances. This goes against the grain, however, because it would mean that they had experienced a purely vaginal orgasm, which I do not believe exists. On the other hand, it is true that quite a large number of men can play with their penises and induce orgasm sensations building up to the point-of-no-return while the penis remains limp. However, seconds before ejaculation begins, stiffening of the penis takes place.) Anyhow, very few women indeed remain unroused once the penis is moving in the vagina, except where the male partner is so loathed that this sets up a psychological block to any sexual response on the woman's part.

Also, as everyone knows, despite the difference in time required by the man and woman to reach a state of arousal, a woman can be directly stimulated into arousal at any time, even when the last thing she was thinking of was love-making right up to the very moment that the mouth was applied to her nipple or the finger to her clitoris. Though unlike the man, she is not subject to automatic arousal because of chemical activity bringing about a physical state that must be relieved; once stimulation starts it is my view that the operation of her hormone production is stepped up, so that she, too, must go through to orgasm in order to relieve the tension this hormone production builds up.

The site of this particular hormone production is the ovaries. In another survey I have recently carried out into British Middle-class Patterns of Sex and Love, 80.6 per cent of my women collaborators have stated that they are sexually stimulated psychogically as they are physically. (I ought to point out that they are young women between the ages of eighteen and twenty-eight.) This is not quite so high as men, who are almost one hundred per cent. (Only those men who are extremely low-sexed are unmoved by pictures of naked women, reading 'sexy' books, thinking 'sexy' thoughts, and so on.) But as the man grows older, he has to rely more and more on direct, physical stimulation of the penis or other highly sensitive erogenous zones. His progress towards orgasm also becomes more easily controllable, though in order to make his technique as near perfect as possible, he must still exert a deliberate influence of will. Nevertheless, the couple are more evenly matched in middle-age than they were when they were younger.

Fortunately, the ovaries continue to produce their sex-drive hormone after the menopause, though a very slow process of decline continues. However, the more experience I gain of this particular aspect of women and love-making, the more I am coming to the opinion that the woman's psychological outlook is a more potent factor in her desire to make love than the functioning of her sex-drive hormone in later years.

Time and again, I have been told about, and have actually observed, post-menopausal women who have completely changed in their attitude towards, and experience of, sex. I have seen this change of attitude described by other writers as a phenomenon; but it is no phenomenon – it is logical and natural.

There are probably more women than not who, no matter how carefully they observe the requirements of the best birth control method – with the possible exception of the Pill – have a deeply embedded fear of an unwanted pregnancy. I am not suggesting that every session of love-making is dominated by this fear but that it is present even if it is not consciously experienced. With the cessation of the menstrual flow, the woman suddenly realises that she has been released from this fear. This is generally a conscious realisation. It is as if a great burden has been lifted from her mind, and she feels that she can now be a much more satisfactory wife sex-wise. Whereas previously she had wanted to enjoy love-making with her husband, now she really can. She can relax as he stimulates her, receive his penis with real ecstasy, and join him in a truly voluptuous climax.

The women to whom this revelation comes are usually those of average sex-drive who would dearly have wished to be the perfect mistress to their husbands, but were held by a psychological intervention stronger than their will to overcome it.

Now released from this bondage they are determined to make up for lost time. They appreciate that the offering of their sex will not be enough. They must woo their husbands, as they did when they were first attracted to one another, in order to be wooed in return.

Imagine such a woman, radiant in her new emancipation, meeting with indifference from a husband who is too lazy to respond. In such a situation we have the seeds of bitterness which will cloud the relationship for the remainder of their years together. I shall be dealing in the next chapter with the practical aspects of the duty of both partners towards one another; but I would like to say here that, in my experience, although the woman more easily withdraws from sex than the man, when she does make up her mind to enjoy it, she does so with a singleness of purpose unmatched by any man. The husband whose wife takes on a new lease of sex after the menopause is an absolute fool, if, out of laziness, fear of his own capacity or any other reason, he does not do his level best to give her what she wants and receive from her what she is so anxious to give.

The menopause itself can be a trying time not only for the woman, but for her husband as well. He must show a patience and an understanding which often has to be Job-like in quality. If I had my way, I would make it statutory for all women embarking on the menopause to be registered and for the husbands of these women to be required, on pain of a large fine, to attend a course of instruction into what is happening physically and is likely to happen psychologically to the woman. Instead of trying to understand, or at least to tolerate, the tears, the complaints, the sighs, the nagging, the headaches, the backaches, too many men dash off to the pub or club.

There is evidence to support the view that the women who suffer – and I mean actually suffer – most from the menopause are those women who for some years before they are overtaken by it have also been overtaken by sexual boredom. The woman who is sexually happy has a far greater chance – serious physical or organic complications apart – of taking the menopause in her stride, of experiencing the least discomfort and the least psychological upset. If a regular sex-life, in which there is the normal variety and adventurousness, is continued throughout the years of the change, she will hardly be aware that it is taking place. She may have the occasional hot flushes, the occasional irregularity of menstruation and perhaps a flooding, or maybe two, but the dread with which so many women so unnecessarily anticipate the menopause will be absent, and her maintenance of her psychological balance will make her passage through the climacteric easy.

In any case, she should never be hesitant in seeking the advice and help of her doctor. I know that it is the attitude of a good many doctors – in the British Isles, at any rate – to regard the menopause of little account. On the other hand, they are liable to put down headaches, spots before the eyes, dizziness, breathlessness and so on in any woman between forty-five and fifty-five to the menopause, whether the woman is going through it or not. How many times does one hear a justifiably irritated woman exclaim, 'I do wish he wouldn't assume that I'm going through the change,' or 'It's no use going to him; he'll say it's "my time of life".' The menopause is inevitable, far too many doctors declare, and has to be put up with.

I have recently written to two of our leading newspapers – neither printed my letter – about the lack of instruction in sexual matters given to our doctors. They are totally unprepared to help their patients who go to them for sexual advice unless there is something amiss with their urino-sexual systems. This is not their fault; no medical course, so far as I am able to discover, includes instruction in the kind of thing that can go wrong without any apparent physical sign.

Let me try to illustrate the kind of thing I mean. Not long ago a doctor telephoned me and asked, 'What can I tell a young chap of twenty-seven who has been married two years and has lost all desire for intercourse? I've told him it's an attitude of mind and that he should snap out of it. He says he's tried, but it's no good.'

'Listen,' I said, 'supposing I rang you up and described a complaint I had in terms as vague as you've just described this young man's complaint. Would you give me a snap diagnosis over the phone?'

'Of course not,' he replied. 'But it's not the same thing. This chap has nothing organically wrong with him. From a medical point of view, there's nothing the matter with him. I only rang up because I know you know something about this sort of thing. He's not ill. I'm positive about that. He has morning erections, he masturbates from time to time, so there's no question of his being impotent; yet he's off making love with his wife.'

'Does that strike you as serious or not?' I asked, beginning to get angry. 'Supposing you were he, what would you feel?'

'Well, I wouldn't bother my doctor with it, because I'd have the sense to know that he hasn't got time to waste on a chap who isn't ill.'

(*He hasn't got time to waste on a chap who isn't ill!*)

'What are you going to do about him?' I asked.

Unless you've got any other answer for him, I'm going to tell him to go home and not to worry. It'll right itself.'

We had a few more words, and in the end I persuaded him to send his patient to a psychiatrist I was able to recommend, who specialises in such problems. In fact, if the doctor had had any training at all in common sexual neuroses he would have been able to help the young man in a few short sessions. As it was, he had to make matters worse for his patient before they could get any better, by referring him to a psychiatrist, which fact alone over-dramatised the young man's condition and undoubtedly made him feel that there was something seriously wrong with him, when there was not.

The same sort of attitude is found, as I say, among far too many doctors towards the menopause. The women are not ill; they are going through a natural process of change; but this does not prevent them from wanting and needing to have sympathetic reassurance, from the one person they know is qualified to give it, that there is nothing wrong. But apart from sympathy there are many things a doctor can do nowadays in the way of prescribing medication that can make the difficulties so much easier. This, of course, presupposes that the doctor keeps up with the latest medical developments. And I have no time for doctors who protest that they are not able to devote the time they feel they would like to give to patients who are ill, and certainly cannot find time to read *The Lancet* and other journals which report the latest medical developments. If they have not the time, then the system under which they are working is wrong and they should seek to change it.

To the patient I would say: 'Don't be fobbed off by a doctor who tells you you are going through a natural change, that you are not ill, and that if you go away and divert your thoughts from the state you are in, all will become right eventually.' I know we still have some way to go before we know everything about hormones, and especially those which regulate our sexual activities, but we have sufficient knowledge now to be able to help those who are experiencing excessive hot flushes and floodings, and a complaint known as dysparaneuia, or painful intercourse, which afflicts woman during and after the menopause.[1] Even help with these problems will make the years of the menopause easier to bear. So if you have, unfortunately, a doctor who takes this line with you, look round for one who is prepared to help, and change to him.

Ideally, the menopause, like everything else to do with sex, whether the best or the worst, is experienced by husband and wife. The wife feels a need, sometimes desperately, to pour out her soul into a sympathetic ear. Another woman's ear – exept that of a woman gynaecologist – is not the best receptacle for the confidences she wants to make, since most women's reactions will be coloured by their own experiences. She cannot share her intimate confidences with another man, and if she cannot share them with her husband, she is indeed deprived. No matter whether the husband knows what the menopause means or entails, or not, let him just listen, and make sympathetic noises; let him take her in his arms; let him put an arm around her shoulders as they sit side by side on the settee; let him jolly her along; let him take her out to a meal, to the cinema, to the theatre; let him buy her a new dress, which they choose together, or give her a present of new underwear; let him forgo a session or two at the pub or club; let him do just a little more about the house than he usually does; above all, let him make her feel

[1] During and after the menopause (and sometimes in the years leading up to it), an insufficient quantity of female sex hormone (estrogen) causes the lining of the vagina to thin out and to become raw and painful when the penis is moved about inside it. There is a simple remedy for this. Estrogen, administered by injection, mouth and/or suppositories in the vagina, will thicken the vaginal-lining and repair the damage.

welcome in his bed. If he will do these things, and anything else he can think of, he will find that not only will things be easier for them both, but that there will be a renewal of the intimacy of the bond of friendship, of companionship, of the lover-relationship which will revive a flagging marriage as a stiff brandy revitalises a flagging body.

There are, in fact, a number of dual responsibilities which are placed fairly and squarely on the shoulders of both at this time of life. Most of them, if not all, have a reciprocal quality. For example, if the husband shows the wife the considerations which I have outlined above, she must do something in return. Ever since I wrote the first words of *Mainly for Wives*, I have insisted in every book, every article, every letter I have written on the subject of sexual physical relationships that the woman has equal sexual responsibilities with the man – and, of course, equal rights.

Let me quote one brief passage from *Mainly for Wives*. 'Whatever the differences in mechanism in the suppression of desire in men and women, if we assume equal partnership, we must also accept the right of the wife to take the sexual initiative whenever she feels like it. Once this is accepted by the husband, the sexual life of both will become richer because now the relationship is a true sharing in which both partners have equal responsibilities.'

Here is summed up the whole of my philosophy on physical sex. It sums up equally well my philosophy not only on all the aspects of sex, but on the marriage relationship as well. Given equal rights, the woman must be willing to give something in return, and not by merely letting her husband use her body, by looking after the home, by cooking his meals and ironing his shirts.

I have had the good fortune to have married two very beautiful women. My first wife was a student of considerable scholarship in the Classics, but from the day I first knew her until the day she died thirty-one years later, she paid the most meticulous care to her figure, her dress and her hair. She would have been beautiful had her scholarly tastes made her eschew waving and setting, nail-varnish, lipstick, rouge and powder. But the construing of Horace and Vergil, Euripedes and Aeschylus did not blind her with their antiquity to the world about her.

My present wife is an artist. She, too, looks as beautiful in her paint-spattered smock as in her mink-collared model suit. She, too, enhances what is already a radiant beauty and a ravishing figure with all the aids that modern beauty-science can provide,

Whether or not I would have been so sexually moved by the sight of them had they come to bed with me in curlers, or slopped about the house in a dressing-gown, I am not quite sure. The fact that I find well-groomed women of certain physical characteristics erotically stimulating might have had something to do with it. But the point I am trying to make is this – both these women could have got away with it beautywise by doing little or nothing to themselves; whereas, both went to enormous pains to keep themselves svelte and attractive!

Many women, I know, find the business of beautifying themselves a terrible chore. I could argue that they owe it to their husbands to accept the chore and make a virtue of it but, in fact, I believe they owe it to themselves. Nothing raises feminine morale, I am constantly being told, more than a hair-do or a new hat. Yet I am also constantly meeting middle-aged women going through or having completed the menopause who wear dull dowdy clothes, whose hair style has nothing on Mrs Noah's, who have sagging chins and cheeks, and hair-covered upper lips, droopy breasts, spreading bellies and prominent bottoms. All that is needed to make these things of the past is a visit to a stylish dress-shop, an hour at a good hairdresser's once a week, an hour and a half at a beauty parlour once a month, a course in tightening sagging muscles at a health and beauty gymnasium, and the determination to keep the muscles tight once they are tight, by a few minutes' exercise a day.[1]

Not only are beauty treatment and mild exercising good for morale, they also keep the body toned up, and with it the sexual system.

[1] One well-known beauty consultant has what is described as Top-To-Toe treatment, which consists of a hair-do, face treatment, neck and shoulder massage, a body massage, manicure, waxing off face and leg hair, and a pedicure. It takes about three and a half hours, and at £7 10s is fantastically cheap. Top-To-Toe is available in every big city in the British Isles.

I, personally, know of nothing more alluring than a soignée, mature woman. You may have your innocent young beauties; for though I can admire them, and was once, when I was their contemporary, sexually attracted to them, now I find them merely beautiful to look at. A beautiful, assured, well-turned-out woman, on the other hand, never fails to attract attention. She has so much to commend her that the young beauty has not. She has calm confidence and above all sexual experience. And I am not speaking about the casual partner. I am speaking particularly to middle-aged men whose wives have taken a new lease of sex with the experience of the menopause over, who have found that sex can at last be something to be carefree about, drained of fear, filled with happiness and fun.

The husband who has had the experience of happy sex-relations from his wedding night to last night will, of course, know what I am talking about. But the husband whose sex in the last few years has gone sour on him is the man who must be capable of reading the signs, of imparting encouragement, and of having the capacity to respond. For if the wife has a duty towards her husband, he has no less a duty towards her.

I have known quite a number of post-menopausal women who have tried to justify their drop-out from sex with the absolutely nonsensical statement that sexual activity is unbecoming in a matron'. Some have also said that a secondary reason for their decision not to have physical sex any more is that they find it ridiculously unromantic making love with a corpulent, wheezing husband, whose penis, never long at the best of times, has become so retiring under its over-hang of belly that it is scarcely able to make contact with the vagina entrance, let alone penetrate it in a straightforward way. The adjustments that have to be made make every episode seem artificial and certainly not spontaneous, natural and romantic.

Apart from the fact that I personally prefer the deliberate to the spontaneous in love-making – since the spontaneous, except on very rare occasions, does not produce the intensely voluptuous sensations which I believe should be the culmination of every episode of love-making – I do agree that most women who make criticisms of this kind have a good deal of justification on their side. Men who let themselves go physically go to seed far more rapidly and more thoroughly than any woman; and one has to admit that the attempts at love-making of a 'paunchy, wheezing lover,' besides being unromantic, are also likely to be ineffectual from both parties' point of view. Men who allow themselves to run to seed are failing as much in their duty to their wives as women are who cannot be bothered to keep themselves physically attractive.

Perhaps it is easier for the man to deteriorate. There are not many men who in their boyhood and youth have not taken a fairly active part in sports and other activities which have relied quite considerably on the use of the stomach muscles. Once these muscles have been used rather more, perhaps, than nature intended them to be, and if, in later life, they are ignored and become flabby, fat forms quickly over and round them and before the man knows where he is, he has a paunch which a weekly round of golf will not control and which an office job encourages.

Fat also forms on other parts of the body. The neck thickens, bulges of fat appear under the arms, the buttocks become more prominent, the breasts take on a discernible feminine formation. Mostly this is due in men, as I have said, to disregard of the muscles in middle-age; whereas in women this is a far less prominent cause, the main source of female fat being the change in function in which the hormones are involved during the menopause, plus overeating which so many women indulge in to compensate for their lessened, or total lack of, sexual activity. Some men also overeat to compensate for their loss of sex, and with both men and women the whole process becomes viciously circular.

Eating is as much a sensuous as it is a physical function. When one was younger the main attraction of eating was to reduce hunger, and it is only as one grows older that one begins to be aware of the sensual delight that food can provide. The reduction of hunger still remains the main function of eating, but the dinner in a good restaurant washed down by a bottle of wine becomes a progressively more prominent feature of living the older one gets. Then when one is deprived of the ecstasy of orgasm, the delight in eating encourages one to eat too much.

Now, you have probably noticed that we use the same words

in respect of sex that we use in respect of food – 'starved,' 'hungry,' and 'satisfied'. We talk about sex-hungry young men, about sex-starved spinsters, a satisfying orgasm and we frequently use the term 'sexual appetite'.

Research has shown that there is a definite connection between nutrition and fertility. It has also shown that there is a definite connection between fertility and the sex-drive. For example, there is a tendency for seasonal cycles to exist in birth, the highest point of which is in February–March, the lowest in September - October. The cycle is related to the naturally larger number of foodstuffs available during the spring months (and the lack of them during the winter months) and the consequent increased vitamin content in the average diet. The entire glandular system of the individual becomes activated by vitamins that are the chemical cousins of hormones and are vital to the proper functioning of the ductless gland network of the body. Vitamin E, for example, affects the function of the pituitary gland, and it is known that vitamins A, C and D, which have a specific equivalent of the various sex hormones, play a considerable part in the treatment of infertility and impotence. Or again, the thyroid gland, which is closely connected with sexual vigour, is totally dependent on the element iodine. Lack of iodine not only produces the swelling in the throat known as goitre, but reduces fertility, the sex-drive and the capacity for erection.

I don't want to go into any great detail here about this interrelation between food-vitamins-hormones, but I think it would be useful for you to know the following facts. Dr A. P. and Dr R. M. Kapadia, writing in the *International Journal of Sexology* 7, have stated their belief, as a result ot their researches, that the tie-up between vitamins and hormones is so close that when, for example, the hormone testosterone is prescribed for the relief of painful menstruation, it is more successful when vitamin D is taken with it. Similarly the hormone's progesterone, when prescribed for threatened abortion, and estradiol, for premenstrual tension, are both more successful when vitamins C and A respectively are also prescribed.

Vitamins, when taken by the mouth in the form of food or tablets, are constructed of such small molecules that they can be absorbed in the bloodstream. On the other hand, hormones produced within the body are not so small molecularly and can be passed into the blood-stream only by digestion. The hormones, however, take part with vitamins in the metabolic action of the body, and thereby influence the way the flesh on the body, is built up. For example, carbohydrate metabolism involves the co-operation of vitamins B_1, B_2 nicotinic acid, insulin, anterior pituitary secretions, corticosterone of the adrenal cortex, and adrenalin. A deficiency of even one of these can bring about serious and far-reaching disturbances of the body economy. B vitamins not only help to arrest cirrhosis of the liver but also, via the liver, play an important role in the metabolism of fats. Many doctors believe that it is the shortage of B vitamins in conjunction with a deficiency of protein that causes the liver cirrhosis among alcoholics.

One of the great hazards of obesity is that the starches ingested for the production of excess weight compete with the liver and the thyroid for vitamin B_1, and impair the functions of both these organs, which are important in sexual potency. (The thyroid affects both fertility and gestation.) In other words, the really fat man or woman not only has a greatly impaired potency and sexual capacity (*i.e.* frigidity) but may lose these characteristics altogether. Since there is a definite connection between potency and sexual desire, the fat man is far less likely to want sex than the thin man, and when or if he does, his performance will not be terribly satisfactory.

Before I pass on, let me make a brief allusion to a point connected with obesity and potency - that is, the ability of the man to have an erection - which I shall be dealing with in more detail when I come to consider impotence. Every *pound* of excess fat increases the distance the blood has to circulate by twenty-two miles. The penis achieves erection by the inflow of blood into the spaces of the spongy tissue. If the man is really corpulent then the fat weakens his general circulation, and not so much blood is available at a given moment for building up an erection. His erection is then only partial, not sufficient to allow the penis to enter the vagina, or completely nonexistent, in which case the man is impotent.

One last point about vitamin deficiencies as they affect sex-drive. A complicating effect of a vitamin B deficiency in a married couple's diet (which they would be likely to experience because they share relatively the same diet) is that the woman would tend to develop, consequent upon excess estrogens (female sex hormones), an increase in sexual desire; while her husband would be the opposite, since an excess of female sex hormones operating on the man overrides the operation of his male sex hormones (androgens). In other words, while the wife wants to make love more often, the husband wants to do so less.

Since it is the sex hormones that are among those most sharply affected by the changes taking place inside our bodies as we move into middle- and old-age anyhow, it is easy to see what an important part diet plays in our sex-lives at a time when other pressures are already being exerted and which affect our sex-drive and our physical capacity for sex. Ideally, every man and woman past fifty should first make a determined effort to get rid of as much of their excess fat as they possibly can – preferably under medical observation – and secondly, to work out a balanced, high protein diet.

Exess fat, besides having the effects I have described above, also creates physical difficulties which affect the couple's ability actually to perform sexual intercourse. Let us take, for example, the couple where the wife is slim or slimmish and the man has a definite paunch. Unless the man has an above-average-length penis, he is going to have difficulty in penetrating the vagina even half-way. This may not worry him unduly because he will have a satisfactory orgasm whether the penis is an inch, four inches, or seven or eight inches inside the vagina. For the woman, however, it is a different matter, because very often there comes a stage in the coupling when she feels a need, which is both biologic and psychologic in origin, for deep penetration. If she is deprived of it, her orgasm may not be as satisfying as she needs it to be. (See *Sex Manners for Men*, pp. 119–120 in the hardback edition, and p. 72 in the paperback edition, for observations on the woman and deep penetration.) This may not matter very much if it happens occasionally, but if she is permanently deprived of deep penetration, she may lose interest in making love altogether. When both partners are fat, this difficulty is accentuated, for a woman with a fat belly almost invariably has prominent buttocks, so that even a rear-entry position is of little avail, when the prominent female buttocks are juxtaposed to the prominent male belly.

The drinking of alcohol also has a definite effect on the ability to make love. A little alcohol may stir sexual desire and, by acting as a stimulant, may liven up even somewhat staid relations. In my view, alcohol acting as a sexual stimulant does so because it diminishes inhibitions. Under its influence we don't care so much about 'what the neighbours might think', and this freedom from psychological restriction allows us to make love with more abandon and more intensely and successfully, where we have not taught ourselves to do so normally without the help of alcohol.

Very definitely, however, intoxication affects a man's potency. When a man is slightly drunk ejaculation occurs earlier than normal because alcohol acts as a local irritant on the urinary passage. Heavier drinking has exactly the opposite effect – it delays ejaculation, and sometimes prevents it from taking place at all. Ejaculation may, in fact, be delayed so long that the penis goes limp and cannot be coaxed back into erection. Indeed, the habitual heavy drinker may not be able to achieve erection at all. Apart from these obstacles to successful intercourse, heavy drinking over a long time causes incurable lesions in the testicles and these prevent the production of sperm, while in women it causes menstrual irregularities.

The difficulty is to know where to draw the line. Once again we see the vicious circle operating. The middle-aged man beset with sexual difficulties which are not of his making probably takes to drink and thereby affects his own capacity for love-making. There is nothing to choose between him and his wife, who was the original cause of the difficulties.

Smoking, too, has a direct bearing on sexual capacity if the smoke is inhaled. An excess of nicotine gets into the blood-stream and affects the circulation, which becomes so sluggish that it prevents full erection, if it does not cause full impotence. It also affects the sexual responses because, like all drugs in small quantities, it acts as a stimulant, though in larger quantities it has a deadening effect on the nervous system which prevents intense orgasmic sensations being experienced, if it does not prevent either erection or orgasm altogether.

Apart from these influences on our sexual lives which our eating and social habits may have, the sexual apparatus itself is subject to various changes which affect its performance. When I was a boy, one of the arguments against masturbation was that it is unnecessary as a means of stimulating development of the sexual apparatus. It is just as well that even the threat of *dementia praecox* (schizophrenia) and of general paralysis of the insane, which adults made to adolescents in the hope of frightening them off masturbation, did not do so, for the argument is a false one. The sexual apparatus needs constant use like every other part of the body, if it is to develop and function properly. Masters and Johnson have discovered that the couple who are sexually more active up to the age of, say, forty, retain the ability to have intercourse – and do so – into old-age; while those who indulged only occasionally lose the ability to have intercourse – and do not do so past middle-age. In other words, the more exercise the sexual apparatus gets between the ages of eighteen and forty the longer it will continue to function in old-age.

The drop-outs from sex are, by and large, in the group who have not made love with any degree of frequency during the peak period (and after) of their sexual lives. If they have not masturbated, either, in middle-age the penis begins to shrink. This shrinkage also affects potency. Similarly, if the seminal vesicles and the prostate, particularly, are not stimulated by fairly frequent orgasms, they lose their maximum capacity for producing their respective secretions, and this is equally true of the testicles and their production of sperms and hormones. Research has shown that there is a very definite relationship between the sex-drive and fertility in the ordinary run of events. That is to say, those whose sexual desire is weak are also likely to be sterile. Although after the wife has passed the menopause the man's fertility rate loses all significance (at least as far as the wife is concerned), the continued proper functioning of his prostate and seminal vesicles remains an important consideration. They must be looked after, and the best way of doing so is by love-making.

If you have decided after reading this that you have become, or are on the verge of becoming, a drop-out from sex and that you would really much prefer not being one, you still have it in your power to take out a new lease of sex. First, see that you have a properly balanced high protein diet, after you have taken the trouble to slim the excess flesh off your body. Regulate your drinking of alcohol and your smoking. With your body as a whole toned up – and I think you will be surprised how greatly your mental attitude to life, and especially your sexual marriage-relationship, will improve if you do – then I would suggest you undertake for a short time the following course of exercises (I am speaking now to the men only) to tone up your sexual equipment.

Exercise 1

Lying just behind the scrotum and surrounding the root of the penis which lies within the body are a number of muscles. When the penis is erect, if these muscles are contracted they cause it to give a jerk upwards towards the belly. These muscles are those which force the semen along the urethra and out of the penis-opening, and when they are doing this, they operate involuntarily, *i.e.* of their own accord.

With a little practice a man can teach himself to contract these muscles voluntarily. It is a useful technique of love-making to be able to do so, for the jumping of the penis in the vagina in this way gives the woman a special thrill; and perhaps in his younger days he was able to do it, but now, because of disuse, has found he can no longer. This first exercise, then, is designed either to develop mastery over this muscle for the first time, or to redevelop control.

The exercise can be carried out with the penis limp, though it will not cause the penis to jump, as it will do when erect. First, find the muscle with a finger placed on the peroneum – the ridge behind the scrotum running to the anus. Press firmly, but not so firmly that it hurts, and then behave as though you were trying to expel the last few jets of urine as you do involuntarily when going to the lavatory.

Because of this finger-pressure, you will have to do the exercise, to begin with, in private. But once you have got a little strength into the muscle and can jerk it slightly, the finger will no longer be necessary. Then you can do the exercise anywhere you like – standing for a bus, sitting in the train, riding an escalator, sitting at your desk, while you are shaving – at any odd moment. No one will be able to tell!

I recommend, even when you can control the muscle vigorously to the extent that when you do so with your penis erect you can lift the tip upwards through an arc of one inch, that you carry out the exercise three or four times a day, contracting the muscles a dozen times each time.

If you find that drops of Cowper's gland lubricating fluid flow from the tip of the penis while you are doing the exercise, don't worry! In fact, you are stimulating these glands, too, by the exercise.

Exercise 2

Rather higher up in the pelvis and surrounding the urethra, is another similar set of muscles which do actually have the function of cutting off the stream of urine. These can be controlled, and strengthened. too. The best way of doing so is by giving them a few extra fillips each time you go to the lavatory after you have expelled the final jet of urine. The fact that they have already gone into motion involuntarily to expel the last jets of urine will make it easier for you to keep their motion going involuntarily.

The following four exercises SHOULD NOT BE CARRIED OUT *by those with a heart condition, or very high blood pressure:*

Exercise 3

Stand with your feet about ten inches apart – more for those with long legs – and brace the legs firmly.

Take a deep breath, and as you do so:

(a) draw the stomach muscles in and up as far as they will go, and
(b) clench the muscles of the buttocks.

While maintaining all three of these tensions – holding breath, drawing in stomach muscles, and clenching the buttocks – rotate the hips one way for so long as holding your breath does not become paiful.

Relax, repeat the tensions and rotate the hips in the opposite direction.

Though the movement involved is not very great, you may find it quite tiring, so do not carry it out last thing at night.

The next three exercises should be carried out naked and near an open window to take advantage of fresh air:

Exercise 4

Lie on your back, arms spread out at an angle of forty-five degrees to the trunk. Press the forearms and palms firmly against the ground. Raise both legs vertically, keeping them straight but not tense, open them so that the feet are about eighteen inches apart. Move the right leg back towards the trunk, four or five inches, and the left the same distance forward. Still keeping the legs straight and the toes pointed move both legs inwards to cross them as far as possible. Return to V position. Now move the left leg back and the right leg forward, and cross them in the opposite position.

Repeat these movements six to eight times. Lower the legs and relax completely until the breathing is normal and all sensations of strain in the thighs have disappeared. If you are reasonably fit, you should be able to do this exercise between six and ten times at any one session, with two sessions a day.

Exercise 5

This exercise should be used on alternate days with exercise 4. On the floor in the same position, raise the legs vertically, then lower the feet until the lower parts of the legs are at right angles with the thighs. Part the knees sideways, keeping the inner edges of the feet together, drawing the feet inwards towards you.

Stop immediately you feel strain in the groin. Return the legs to the original position before repeating. This exercise, which becomes easier and more rhythmic with practice, should not be repeated more than ten times a session, with two sessions a day.

Exercise 6

Stand three or four feet, depending on your height, from a table, bed-rail, or other firm support of approximately waist height. Lean forward with the legs straight, placing the palms of the hands on the edge of the support, with the arms extended. You should balance yourself so that your weight is more or less equally distributed between the feet and the hands. With the buttock muscles tensed, and without bending either arms or legs, thrust the pelvis forward and upward as far as possible until you feel a slight strain in the small of your back. Withdraw in the same arc, and repeat continuously, gradually working up to forty of fifty arcs at each session, with two sessions a day.

The two sessions a day need only be carried out until you feel you have got all the parts alluded to in thorough working order. But unless you lose interest altogether, in which case the muscles and other organs will in time lose their tone, you should carry them out every other day. You will find that they are not only good for their special purpose, but keep the stomach muscles taut and so reduce the paunch.

There are no comparable exercises for women, possibly because they have fewer moving parts, so to speak. Women however, should have a routine of general exercises, designed to keep muscles flexible and taut, and the fat down. With their general body tone, their sexual apparatus will stay in good shape.

You should now be in good fettle to acquire a new lease of sex.

6: A New Lease of Sex

From this point on I shall take it for granted that both of you have made up your minds to renew or refurbish your experience of sex. As I said earlier, even if you did not treat it seriously when you were younger, and used intercourse merely as a means of relieving tension rather than as a symbol of your love for one another, there is no earthly reason why you should not start off on the right foot now.

First of all, I think you should try to talk about it with one another. This may be difficult for you to begin with, and it is a pity that this first step should present a problem of communication. But our generation has never been very communicative about sex. Reticence, inhibition and an embarrassing lack of acceptable words have made us doers rather than talkers; and yet, you know, wherever you find a sexually happy pair, you will find a pair who have been able to talk to one another about their desires, and their experiences in the most intimate terms.

The question of vocabulary, I know, is a very difficult one. I have said elsewhere that I wish to goodness the four-letter Anglo-Saxon words could come back into our ordinary everyday speech as the respectable words they started out as. I think we are moving towards it; but *we* can't wait for it. Still, the really sexual words we need are few, and though we may find ourselves a little awkward using them at first, I think we shall find that soon we can say *penis* and *vagina*, *clitoris* and *testicles* without wanting to giggle. I can see no reason at all to object to *balls* for testicles, if testicles seems too artificial; though I have a sneaking feeling that many women who have been used to using any sexual words at all may find testicles easier.

In speech I would shun *orgasm.* I always smile at the thought of a husband in the middle of intercourse inquiring of his wife, 'Are you approaching orgasm, dear?' when what he really means is, 'Are you coming, dear?' or 'Have you come?' 'To bring off' is also natural. to my way of thinking: 'Bring me off, dear!' and 'Shall I bring you off now?' Sexual intercourse and the sex-act, coitus and copulation are avoidable words, too. 'To make love' or 'love-making' are much better phrases and sound quite natural in speech. 'Make love to me,' or 'Will you make love to me?', or 'Shall we make love?' come as tidily off the tongue as anything, and the phrase is as descripitive as it is euphonistic. In writing, in order to differentiate between 'fore-play' and the last phase of love-making when the penis has been put into the vagina, I use 'coupling'. And I am quite sure that when a wife has reached the stage of stimulation when she is ready to receive the penis, she won't say 'Penetrate me, darling', but 'Come into me, darling'.

I think I have said enough to illustrate that it is possible to talk about sex in everyday words and phrases that need not embarrass even the most modest of wives. However, one must realise that even though every day words may be used, the fact that the speaker knows they are referring to sex may still make it difficult for her to use them. Why I should put the emphasis on the wife, I don't know; for many husbands are just as withdrawn when it comes to speaking about sex to their wives. The only advice I can give is: it is essential for a couple to be able to talk to one another about sex if they are to derive any real benefit from sex itself. That they expect sex to benefit them in their middle- and old-age is surely the main, if not the sole, reason for their attempting to take it up again. Believe me, it is possible for any couple to overcome their inhibitions to the extent of talking about sex, but you will have to work it out for yourselves. It is the first test of the real intention of a couple to rehabilitate their sex-lives that they succeed in this. But there is no need to set yourselves too high a literary standard. A word or two in the dark – 'Come into me', 'Are you coming?' 'Was it all right?' – will break the ice, and if helped along by gestures such as taking the partner's hand and placing it on the breast – or penis

– and whispering, 'Play with me there' It should not be too difficult to establish a simple two-way communication.

Normally, I am dead against making love in the dark because it deprives the couple of so much stimulus in the way of looking at the partner's body, and especially his or her face on which, unless the caresses are really having no effect at all, traces of what they are experiencing must be reflected. Until you have established whatever sex vocabulary you decide upon, however, you should not seek the dark's protection permanently. sex can never be enjoyed thoroughly unless it has eyes.

At the same time that you are setting up your communications, you should also be observing your own and your partner's responses to love-play and coupling. The sort of things you will want to know are: how often do you feel the urge to make love and how often does your partner? Have there been any changes in his/her sensitive zoning since the early days? Are there any forms of caress which are especially stimulating to him/her? Is there any position for coupling which seems to be particularly effective? Does your partner seem satisfied with his/her orgasm? and so on. In the beginning watch, and note. Later, when you are able to talk, talk about them as fully as you can.

When you first got married, were you able to overcome your natural modesty and accustom yourself to seeing one another naked? I think you would be surprised to know the number of couples I have encountered who are still inhibited in this way. They dress and undress with their backs to one another, they lock the bathroom door, and their fore-play and coupling is carried out through an interfering haze of nightdress and pyjamas.

With the middle-age figure's almost certain blemishes one can understand a certain reticence in appearing naked before your partner. But you really should stop this Victorian nonsense of the hand over the penis and balls and vagina and breasts, and the little yelp of protest when you are surprised. Your partner has a right to know by sight the body with which she is expected to share her sex and you have the same right. Perhaps, if you have let yourself go physically to seed, letting your partner have a good look at you will encourage you to take your figure in hand more vigorously.

And for heaven's sake, do get rid of your night-clothes when you make love. This is advice I urge on all young couples, for the sensual response of naked flesh against naked flesh is one of the most powerful stimulants there is. Nowadays, you cannot afford to overlook any aid to sensation you can think of, or that comes your way. In these early stages, until you have established a new rhythm of sex, you must use, and deliberately so, every aid you can devise and summon. Later, you will find they come to you naturally, and though to begin with you may experience a reluctance to be so cold-blooded about it, you really have no choice. You really had no choice when you first got married, if you wanted your love-life to be a successful one. Maybe one of the chief reasons, if not the chief, for your getting to the state you have was because you did not take the trouble to find out then what you are trying to discover now. If you had experimented, and done so thoroughly, with caresses, adventurous fore-play and exciting positions, you probably would not have come to the pass from which you are going to extricate yourself now.

Whenever I am shown, proudly, round a friend's or a neighbour's house and see twin beds in the master bedroom, then I know for sure that the sex-life of my hosts is not an entirely happy one, if it exists at all. *Single beds are for single people.* Another of Chartham's Laws would compel married couples to sleep in double beds!

Sex in a single bed – except *faute de mieux* and with the blazing ardour of youth or of exceptionally long abstinence – is doomed before it starts. In middle-life and in English houses it is the most powerful deterrent to sex there is. Though it generally falls to the man to play the gallant, you cannot ask it of either partner that he/she deserts his bed to make love to you in the knowledge that, if all has gone well with your caresses and coupling, just when you are feeling friendliest and most contentedly relaxed, you must return to a cold empty bed, leaving your partner alone, when you want to feel her relaxed in your arms and she wants to snuggle up to your glowing warmth.

In any case, you have got to have room to manoeuvre in order to make love successfully. Three feet six inches is no room at all, and if the bodies are plump ones or large ones, it is minus. The wife must lie on the hard edge of the bed if she is the predominantly passive partner, and even when she does, how many husbands, I wonder, have not got frozen bottoms from exposure, by having to expose them over the opposite edge in order to bend down to caress the partner's breasts and body with mouth and tongue? If you have relegated yourselves to single beds promote yourselves at once; relegate them to a guest-room, though even that is not kind, if a husband and wife are ever to be your guests, and splash out with a new four-foot-sixer with a mattress that is firm but comfortable for yourselves!

If you are going to buy youselves a new bed – and it makes a good start to a new enterprise such as the one on which you are engaged – get one that has a solid foot-board. You will find it useful in your love-making if you carry out certain suggestions of mine which I shall come to later.

If you more or less gave up sex some time ago, it was very likely from boredom. Boredom could arise only from two causes: either that you were lazy and took the easiest way of bringing yourself off, or, though you might be interested in making each orgasm a worthwhile experience, your imagination did not suggest a variety of techniques for doing so and you did not know you might have got help from books.

Now that you are making a new start, you will be able to avoid making the same mistake again. On the other hand, your task is a bit easier, because you won't be able to use all the techniques you might have in your earlier days, by reason of the physical limitations imposed on you by your age. At the same time you must have a variety of techniques on which to ring the changes in order to prevent boredom creeping in again.

I am dead against setting out various techniques of fore-play step by step, firstly because one of the recipients of such a programme of caresses may not respond fully to a specific programme although another may be brought to a state of near sexual delirium within a few minutes by the same scheme of hand, mouth and tongue stimulation. What I would like to do, however, is to suggest a few caresses in a few places which are particularly rewarding with regard to sensation. These you can mix with the caresses you recall from former days, remembering that the permutations of even eight or nine will give you a very wide variery of programmes.

May I speak first to the wife?

A great deal is going to depend on your attitude to your love-making, whether or not you successfully rehabilitate sex in your lives. With few exceptions, and then I believe it is not fundamentally natural, men are much coarser-grained than women, They have certainly different standards of modesty, which, I think, is demonstrated by the fact that whereas the majority of men do not hesitate to be naked in front of other men, should the occasion demand, there are few women who do not have some degree of reluctance in undressing completely even among members of their own sex. Men, too, are much more prone to the risqué joke and dirty story than women are – I believe, though I cannot say so for certain, since I have never been admitted to the most intimate feminine circles, the counterparts of those stag gatherings where often the vocal atmosphere goes through all the tone-range of blue and purple.

This coarseness of speech with regard to sex is only one aspect of the man's more open and general approach to it. He is, by and large, much franker, and I have some ideas about why so, too. A woman can be sexually roused, and though naked, can be seen to be only if examined very closely indeed. But when the man is roused, it is difficult for him to hide his erect penis even when he is fully clothed. The erect penis is the sign of his aggressive sexuality, just as the protective folds of the woman's vaginal lips are the symbol of her sexual good taste.

This is no place to pursue such thoughts, but the little I have said may give you some inkling of what I am trying to get at. If not actively dissuaded by you, your husband will be able to rehabilitate his sex-life more easily than you may be able to rehabilitate yours, because of these different standards of modesty and the man's more direct approach to sex.

However, there are some men who, knowing that many women still regard sex as a necessary evil, curb their natural forthrightness and become hesitant in making any sexual approach at all to their wives. The last thing they want to do is to be regarded by their wives as sexual ogres or dirty old men, and they tend to go to the other end of their pendulum swing and make no sexual approach at all, if they are once rebuffed.

A good deal depends on you, therefore. However direct, however unbecoming you find his sexual suggestions to be, unless he is outrageously uncouth, bear with him; that is, if you really do not want to have anything more to do with sex.

Poor old you! Why is it you who always has to make the allowances?

But is it really?

Sex is fundamentally the most intimate of all human relationships. If it is worth anything at all, and particularly if you look on it as the visible symbol of your love for one another, then there is no reason at all why there should not be absolute frankness of thought and speech and deed between the two partners in the privacy of their sex-rooms. Unless you can accept your husband's approaches, whatever they may be – so long as he is not a pervert – in no matter what form he makes them, don't waste his time. Tell him succinctly that you can't be bothered with his sex, and that you'll let him divorce you, if he wants to.

There should be no holding back at all between the loving couple, in the whole realm of sex, whether it be in discussion or in action. In every book I write it seems to be that I just have to point out to women: if you really love your husband and regard love-making as the physical expression of your love, there is nothing outside out-and-out perversions that a couple may not discuss and do with absolute propriety and ethical soundness.

Far too many women have got it into their heads that coupling in any other position except the face-to-face-man-above is 'not nice', is 'wrong', is even perverted.

Let me say straightaway that no love-making that concludes with the penis in the vagina can possibly be perverted. Yet the number of women I have met who refuse to allow their husbands to go into them from behind because 'it is wrong – like the animals – degrading' is surprising.

There are some very funny ideas going about about perversions. Apart from violent sadism and masochism, there is nothing a man and woman can do together which is perverted unless *it is to the total exclusion of concluding intercourse with the penis in the vagina*, no matter from which side or from what angle. In other words, if a man and woman bring each other off by masturbation every time they make love, and never, never come with the penis in the vagina, that is perversion; if, on the other hand, they bring one another off occasionally by hand or mouth, that is not perversion.

A lot of women dislike engaging in mouth-genital caresses. (When the man stimulates the woman's clitoris and vaginal entrance with his mouth and tongue, the caress is known as *cunnilingus*; when the woman kisses, licks and sucks the man's penis, the caress is known as *fellatio*.) Both cunnilingus and fellatio have been practised by men and women for many thousands of years, perhaps since prehistoric days, but certainly since history was recorded in one form or another, by drawings or writing; not just by peculiar men and women, but ordinary men and women, not occasionally but frequently, not in small numbers, but throughout whole communities.

If a woman is totally honest, she has to admit that the caress of her husband's lips and tongue on her clitoris, vaginal-lips, outer and inner lips, and her vaginal-entrance is among the most exquisitely sensuous, voluptuous sensations she can experience. May I assure you that men find fellatio equally rapturous.

I think many women's refusal to fellate their husbands is not moral but physical. They fear that their husbands will come in their mouth, or that the semen and the Cowper's gland fluid have an unpleasant taste. The Cowper's gland lubricating fluid, besides being transparent, is also odourless and tasteless and the semen, too, has no taste. In any case, there are very few husbands who would not promise their wives that they will give them ample warning of their coming.

Most men want to be fellated, but not necessarily to orgasm. They prefer the caress to be used as part of love-play, to build up the tension-sensations, so that when they come with the penis in the vagina, the final sensations of orgasm are magnificent – as they rarely fail to be after love-play of this kind.

You ought to know that many men quite frequently have an overwhelming desire to be fellated. Just because your husband has not told you so, it does not mean that he is one of the odd-men-out in this respect. Probably he has been dying for you to do it to him, and hasn't liked to ask you – quite simply – 'Kiss my penis,' 'Suck my penis,' or 'Go down on me, please,' because he has felt you might object or be offended.

For all their coarseness where sex is concerned most men have a wish not to offend their wives. One of the things you must make quite plain to him now is that you won't be offended by anything he wants to do to you or have you do to him; within reasonable bounds, that is, and those bounds include cunnilingus and fellatio, and even wearing his boots to make love to you in, if he has this mild complex, and even gentle beating if he is mildly masochistic, though I think you could reasonably object to mild sadism, if you are not mildly masochistic yourself.

If what holds you back is the fear of receiving his semen in your mouth, tell him so. He may not want to come, as I have said, except in the normal way; but I am sure that in any case he will give you his solemn promise not to do what you do not want him to do. But even if he does accidentally, I doubt very much if you would ever be able to tell that he has come, except by the throbbing of his penis. When a man and woman are sexually roused, you may have noticed, they make abnormally large amounts of saliva. Cunnilingus and fellatio are not only highly stimulating to those who are receiving the caresses but to those who are making them, and your mouth will be so full of saliva that you will not be able to tell that semen has been deposited in it.

If you have the urge to be the recipient of cunnilingus, do not fail to tell your husband. I think you will be surprised at the alacrity with which he will comply and the pride in the fact that you have asked him. All you have to say is, 'Kiss me down there,' or 'Lick me', or 'Go down on me'.

I have dwelt at some length on mouth-genital caresses and particularly on fellatio, because if you do accept it as an ordinary caress, I am sure you will be surprised how useful it is going to be. As your husband gets older he becomes more and more immune to pyschological stimuli. That is to say, he won't get erections any more when he looks at pictures of beautiful girls, or even at beautiful girls themselves, or, I regret to say, when he looks at you, and even when he fondles you. *This is absolutely normal for many men over fifty-five, and quite a number of men over forty-five find themselves in the same boat.* He won't usually be entirely without an erection; and he will need some slight encouragement.

Usually fondling of the penis is enough, but if you want to do a really good job fellate him. There will be occasions when he won't even start off with a partial erection; then fellatio is the only sure-fire remedy.

This inability to achieve spontaneous erection is nothing to do with impotence or partial impotence. It has its origins in the lessening response of the sexual motor to spontaneous firing. We need to pull out the choke – in this case fellatio. Once the engine has started it runs quite happily.

Talking of this and impotence, it is essential that you should understand your husband's little difficulties, and, above all, be sympathetic towards them. If you allow yourself to be irritated by his failures, or let your irritation be apparent, you will only make matters far worse.

This is particularly true of those twin male bugbears – premature ejaculation and retarded ejaculation. Premature ejaculation is when the man cannot control his progress towards orgasm, and gets so worked up himself, just by stimulating his partner, that he comes at the slightest provocation, usually immediately on getting his penis into the vagina, and sometimes before he gets it that far. The snag about it is that he leaves his partner wet and dry and she then can only come off if she is stimulated manually. It is regarded mostly as an affliction of the young and over-eager. Unfortunately not enough research has been done into its origins to know what is the exact cause of it. Certainly lack of psychological control is contributory, and certainly extremely sensitive nerves in the penis-tip and frenum play quite a large part, with younger men, at any rate. But why, after successful years of love-making when there has never been any sign of it, it should suddenly afflict men who did not suffer from it when they were younger is something of a mystery. For young men who write to me for help when it upsets them, I recommend one of the anaesthetising creams that are now available which have the effect of deadening the nerves involved temporarily and delay coming off. If your husband would like to know about these creams, and he writes to me care of the publishers of this book, I will give him the particulars. The creams work very well.

Retarded ejaculation is a much more difficult problem to

counteract. It occurs when it takes a man a very long time to come – if he manages to come at all. As a general rule the ability to delay coming off is looked on with favour because it gives the woman time to come, not once, but two or three times - what we call a multiple-orgasm – which is more satisfying; and a good many men also deliberately delay ejaculation in order to draw out the pleasurable sensations. But there is a point at which any further delay sets up tension that, if not relieved, becomes painful. Young and healthy men experience retarded ejaculation from time to time, but this generally happens when they have had several sessions of love-making to orgasm in quick succession. In older men it is usually psychological in origin; they are so anxious to avoid premature ejaculation that they set up counters to it in their minds, and get so carried away that instead of coming too soon, they cannot come at all – and suffer physical hell because of it. For though they will lose their erection after a time, the sensation of tension remains. If the complaint seems to be permanent, it may be due to a blockage of the ejaculatory duct of the prostate, inflammation of the seminal vesicles, or constriction of the back part of the urethra. Make your husband see a specialist urologist at once, for though all these causes can be corrected, they must have expert attention.

While we are on the subject of possible temporary male failures connected with erection, there is the possibility of your husband losing his erection after he has gone into you but before either of you has had a chance to come. This, perhaps, is the most distressing of all male failures, because it overtakes him so suddenly, and has happened before he appreciates what is occurring. If the erection goes so completely that the penis slips out of the vagina, there is nothing else for it but to try to stimulate it back to erection again. Before you can fellate the penis, it will be necessary for him to get out of bed and wash it, because it will be covered with your vaginal secretions, which you will, in all likelihood, find distasteful. Should this happen – I mean the penis slipping out of the vagina – before you begin to attend to him ask him to bring you off by one means or another in the shortest possible time. While he is attending to you, fondle him. The psychological reaction to his knowing that he is bringing you off may go some way to reinstating his erection, and this combined with your fondling of his penis may do the trick, so that as soon as you have come he may be able to go back into you, which will give you the benefit of prolonged orgasm sensations.

More often than not, however, the penis, though limp, does not quickly shrink back to its normal limp size, but remains quite large, though soft, and does not slip out of the vagina. If you act quickly you may be able to restore his full erection within a few seconds, in the following way.

If you are using the man-above position, and he is lying inside your legs, change position so that his legs are lying outside yours and he is gripping your thighs between his. At the same time you should grip his penis as hard as you can with the muscles of your vaginal-entrance. (If you have not learned how to do this I will explain it presently.) If your arms are long enough – and they should be except when the couple are extravagantly ill-matched – reach a hand round over his buttocks and feel his scrotum carefully. (Treat his scrotum and its contents very tenderly at all times, won't you, because they are always very tender. Pain inflicted here at this moment may have the reverse effect of what you are trying to do.) His scrotum, by the way, should be lying on top of your closed legs. It will be what I describe as tight; that is to say, it will not be loose, but contracted as it is when he plunges into cold water; the scrotum always goes tight when the man has an erection, and does not go loose again until some time after he has come off.

Find the spot on the scrotum above the balls, as near to the bottom of the penis as possible, and grip it firmly – but not nipping it so as to cause pain – and pull it away from you quite hard, at the same time gripping the penis with the vaginal muscles, to avoid pulling it out of you. This has the effect, if you pull hard enough, of pulling on the penis skin and stretching the frenum, where most of the nerves are which control erection and orgasm. The effect of stretching the frenum, probably painful (not excessively so, but it should hurt somewhat) is to stimulate these nerves and within a very short time erection may be restored. The effect of your gripping his penis with your vaginal muscles will be to maintain your own progress towards orgasm, and with good fortune, a coupling that might easily have had to be abandoned can be brought to a satisfactory conclusion agreeable to both. But you must act quickly; either as soon as you find you can't feel the penis inside you, or your husband tells you he has lost his erection, which he can do in such terms as, 'I've lost it,' or 'I've gone small', or 'It's gone soft'. Never at any time is it more essential for husband and wife to be able to communicate precisely with one another, as it is in coupling, and especially in coupling which, experience has taught, can be precarious.

Stretching the frenum in this way is also quite successful, in many cases, in resolving retarded ejaculation. Since the penis will be stiff there is no need to change positions so as to grip it with the vaginal muscles; in fact, it is better not to do so. To reach the scrotum, slip your hand between your two pubic areas and take hold of it in the spot I indicated above. Pull downwards at the same time as your husband pushes his penis upwards into you. The pressure of his pubic area on your general clitoral area will keep your own sensations going despite the intervention of your hand, if you keep it a little to one side.

(Quite a number of men, by the way, occasionally use this method of stretching the frenum as an alternative method of masturbation. It is quite likely that your husband will have done so once or twice in his life-time, and probably as a boy or young man, and he will be able to show you what to do if you haven't quite followed my description.)

By the way, the best method of taking hold of the scrotum is to ring your thumb and forefinger fairly tightly round it and pushing away from you, with his balls under the palm of your hand, as though you were trying to squeeze them out of the bag.

I am being constantly surprised by the number of men who do not realise, until they discover it accidentally, how sensitive to stimulation the scrotum is to very light strokes of the palm of a woman's hand. Begin at the base and very lightly draw the palm up over the scrotum, just brushing it. If you continue slowly with the same kind of touch up over the penis until you reach the penis-tip, you will surprise your partner, if the caress is new to him, by the intensity of the sensations with which you will provide him.

If you do not know them already, go exploring your husband's body with him as your guide, in order to discover his most sensitive spots. (You should co-operate with him in the same way.) Ten to one he will not reveal one very sensitive spot, simply because he is unaware of it. This is the ridge situated behind the scrotum extending from the base of the penis to the anus. It is called the *peroneum*, and is extremely sensitive to light and firm stroking with the fingertips or tongue.

You probably have no idea of your expectation of physical sexual life. Let me give you a few brief particulars, based on the researches of Masters and Johnson. Your nipples will become hard and erect when you are sexually roused by the mouth or fingers of your husband until you are in your late seventies. Your clitoris will also respond with erection and behave exactly as it did when you were first married, except that it may require longer stimulation. Your outer vaginal lips will *not* swell and open like they did earlier when you are past the age of fifty-five or sixty; this is due to the reduced hormone levels after the menopause. Your inner vaginal lips will continue to swell a little throughout the sixties, but they will gradually lose the power to do so. Bartholin's gland, which lubricates your vaginal area, gradually ceases production of its slippery fluid, until it has ceased doing so altogether, by the time you reach your seventies.

It is in the vagina that the greatest changes take place after the menopause. I have already spoken about the thinning and smoothing of the vaginal walls which may give rise to pain when the penis is put into the vagina; and I have also told how it can be thickened again, and the cause of the pain removed, by injections of hormone as prescribed by your doctor. This is not likely to occur until your sixties, and will get progressively worse in your seventies, but can always be put right by booster injections.

The vagina also becomes shorter and narrower as you grow older. Your husband can always adjust to your length – with your help – and the narrowing is really a bonus, for it will help you to have closer contact with the penis. This will heighten the penis-vagina sensations for both of you.

Before going on to the womb, may I explain briefly how you can develop the muscle at the entrance of the vagina to which

I referred earlier, so that you can contract and relax it at will. Some women have already taught themselves how to do this when they were younger, but it is surprising how many women do not know that they can control this muscle – which contracts in varying degrees involuntarily, when you have an orgasm – in the same way that the man can control the muscles that make his penis jerk. You will find it easier, I believe, if instead of using a finger, as some suggest, you use a smooth round object, like one of those round ebony rulers, though anything that is round and without sharp edges will do. Anyhow, whatever it is you use, it should be about four inches round, with a rounded end if possible – if not, be very careful how you use it – and it must be clean. Having lubricated it with saliva, insert it carefully about two inches into the vagina and then try to grip on it with the vagina entrance.

At first it may feel that you cannot budge the muscle at all. But don't give up! It will begin to respond after a time, and within a week or two of five minutes' practice a day, you should have the sensation that you are actually gripping the instrument tightly with the vagina-entrance. When you reach this stage, use a smaller – I should say a less thick – instrument like a fountain pen and practise until you feel you are gripping on that. When you reach this stage you will have full control of the muscle. You grip and relax; by the way, you do not try to keep up a continuous grip.

Besides being useful for holding the half-limp penis in the vagina and helping to stimulate it back to erection, it is also a useful manoeuvre in cases of retarded ejaculation. The wave-like gripping of the muscle about the base of the penis is very stimulating to the man when his penis is erect, and I have known two cases of retarded ejaculation cured almost entirely by the action of this muscle. When you have perfect control of the muscle you should continue to have two or three gripping sessions – without using any instrument – a week, to keep the muscle toned up.

The womb also becomes much smaller after the menopause. This is not likely to cause any repercussions in your sex life. It will still contract when you come off, and add its sensations to the others.

Actually, then, as you grow older, your sexual responses will not change very much. Lucky you! For you are in a much superior position to your husband, whose responses may be quite definitely affected by encroaching age.

Let us see what happens to you, gentlemen.

I will deal with your most important old-age problem – in some detail – in the next chapter, though I have already said something about the causes of impotence already. Though very few men know it, your nipples become erect when you are sexually excited, like the woman's do. This nipple-erection is one of the first casualties of ageing, but it is no loss, for only a fortunate few, mostly of really highly-sexed men, have any sensations to fondling or sucking of the erect nipples. Mind you, not all men lose nipple-erection, and when it is maintained it generally lasts much longer than it did when you were younger.

No matter how quickly you have been able to come to erection when you were younger, you will definitely slow up, though gradually, after fifty-five. I have already warned your wife that she will nearly always have to help you to obtain erection; but even if she is really skilful in caressing your penis, you will still respond much more slowly. Don't worry how long it may take to make you erect; the main thing is to have an erection, and you will be defeating your ends if you begin to worry about it.

The testicles get a little bit smaller with age, but not discernibly so. The penis, on the other hand, does have a definite tendency to shrink. This shrinkage can be counteracted by three or four minutes' exercise and massage a day, or every other day. If you are uncircumcised, pull the foreskin right back over the ridge. With the thumb just under the ridge, and the forefinger and second finger at the base of the frenum, grip the penis and stretch it upwards and outwards away from the body until you feel a mildly painful pulling sensation in the penis. Hold it there until you count fifteen seconds, then let it relax. Repeat this, say a dozen times daily. Ideally this should be followed by five minutes hand massage of the penis, lubricated with a soft cream, like theatrical cleansing cream, which is easily bought in most towns and cities of any size, or by post from firms which sell grease-paint and other actor's aids. I hope you will be able to bring your penis to full erection within five minutes. When you have, keep up the massage – as though you were masturbating – until you feel you will come if you go on. If you don't obtain an erection, continue with the massage for five minutes. The object is to stimulate the blood-flow into the penis, and thereby not only counteract the shrinkage, but tone up the erectile tissues so that the erection is achieved more easily and firmly. As I have said, this exercise and massage should be carried out daily if you can find the time, and is particularly important from the middle-sixties onwards.

You will also notice a difference in ejaculation. When you were a young man, after the point-of-no-return had been reached, you could feel the semen being jerked through the urethra. You will no longer have this feeling after sixty; but it is no loss, and in no way affects the sensations of coming off. Previously, too, the semen left the penis in between five and eight spurts. Now there may be only one spurt, and the rest may trickle out of the penis in a continuous flow; or it may leave the penis in a continuous flow from beginning to end. Some men lose their warning sensations, too, the semen suddenly appearing and taking them by surprise. I suppose more than half the men over sixty-five experience this. None of these things affects the quality of the orgasm sensations very much; and though you probably will not have the intense orgasm you had when you were twenty-five, they will be entirely satisfying.

What I have told your wife about her co-operating with you applies to your co-operation with her. You must find out what helps her most, exploring her body with her as your guide trying to discover the places on it which respond most to caresses, and the type of caresses which draw out the most intensely pleasurable sensations.

Now a word about frequency. You will undoubtedly find as you grow into your late sixties and seventies that your sex-drive won't operate quite so often. Your wife may quite easily want to make love more often than you do. Whenever she shows signs of it, but you don't happen to have the urge, *never refuse to co-operate with her!* Encourage her to be sex-mad, if you like. If you can't actually couple with her because of absent erection even under the most skilful caresses from her, concentrate on bringing her off with those caresses which will provide her with an orgasm as near to 'coupling orgasm' as possible; and I think you will find you will achieve this best by going down on her. But I also think you will be surprised at the number of times you can have a normal coupling though you haven't felt like it to begin with. How often? Well, if at seventy you can come or feel you want to come once a week, you are doing pretty well; once a fortnight is not bad either. How often doesn't really matter; what really matters is the quality of the experience.

I have said earlier that tiredness as an excuse for not making love just does not wash. On the other hand, as you get older, neither of you should attempt to make use of positions that require acrobatics or positions that are at all tiring. Now, I have said over and over again that boredom is the greatest enemy of sex and you must have a repertoire not only of caresses but of positions which will allow you to permutate, to ring the changes. The variety which half a dozen or nine coupling positions can bring into your sexual experience is wide, and I am going to suggest to you a few which are not only effective but at the same time not tiring. By the way, I hope by the time you have got as far as this that you have made a really determined effort to get rid of that excess flesh. Paunches, both male and female, have an awkward tendency to get in the way and to prevent really close physical intimacy in most of the positions.

If either of you is still a bit corpulent, you will get the closest penis-vagina contact with the woman above, kneeling. The man lies on his back and the woman kneels astride him, just above his penis. When she has put the penis into her, she sits down on his upper legs.

Before I go any further, I would like to come back to my suggestion about having a bed with a solid footboard. This can be helpful with both partners in several positions, in this way. If the most active partner lies far enough down the bed so that his/her soles press firmly and quite flat against the footboard, the actions he/she is required to make need not be so vigorous. By pressing the soles against the footboard, a leverage is obtained which allows the pelvic movements to be greatly reduced and yet be just as effective. If you try it out you will see what I mean.

If the man has so arranged it that he is pressing the soles of his feet firmly against the footboard – rails will not do – when he thrusts with his pelvis he need do so only so slightly that his buttocks do not leave the bed; in fact they need not move at all. This means they will not be tensed, which is the cause of the tiring of more vigorous in-and-out thrusting momements. If you used this position when you were younger, the woman probably made an up-and-down movement on the penis. This can be quite tiring. It is scarcely tiring at all, however, if the woman, taking hold of one of the man's hands with both of hers, instead of raising herself up and down, rocks backwards and forwards, at the same time that the man maintains contact with her vaginal-entrance and ridge by the slight upwards movement of his pelvis, as I have suggested, With his free hand, he should stimulate either a nipple or the clitoris.

The soles pressed firmly against the footboard also help to reduce the need for more vigorous movement in the traditional man-above position. Instead of making in-and-out thrusting movements, he will find that he can make rhythmic rotary movements with his pelvis, so that his pubic bone never breaks contact with her clitoral area. Only when she has come and he wishes to bring himself off, need he begin to use thrusting movements, and it is quite surprising how much less tiring these are when made with the soles of the feet pressed against the footboard.

As a variation on the man-above position, instead of having both legs inside the woman's, he places one outside one of hers. His inside foot should press against the footboard. In this position the penis lies in the vagina obliquely, and its movements at this angle provide sensations for the woman which she does not have if the penis goes straight into the vagina. The man can either make the rotary movements with his pelvis which I have just described or make long, slow thrusting movements, but the point is, that with his foot making a purchase on the footboard, he does not have to tense his buttock-muscles, nor make such use of his pelvic muscles, both of which are tiring.

A variation of the woman kneeling above the man is for her to have her back to him. If she leans forward a little, and places the palms of her hands on her knees, she can go forward and back on the penis. In this position, the penis is bent forward against its natural angle, and the top of the shaft is thus pressed hard against the upper vaginal wall, which provides extremely pleasant sensations for the woman. The man should make the following movement: with his feet pressed firmly against the footboard, in rhythm with his partner's movements, he makes a motion as though sliding back and forth on the bed. This he does by starting off with the knees very, very slightly bent, and then pushing with his feet and relaxing, pushing and relaxing. He need move only two or three inches along the bed at most, but this is sufficient to bolster the woman's movements, and so both come out of the encounter much less tired.

If you are both quite slim, you can couple lying facing one another on your sides. You will have to sort out the positions of your legs, so that you get the best penis-vagina contact. But at least one foot of each partner should press against the footboard. I never think this is a very satisfactory position, but there are some who find it rewarding.

Another side position is that in which the woman presents her back to her partner. But here again the couple have to be fairly slim for the penis to get in far enough to give the woman worthwhile sensations. The man should press his lower leg against the footboard and put the other over the top leg of the woman.

For variety, there is a woman-above position which is not at all tiring and uses only part of the bed. The man lies with his back on the bed, his buttocks protruding over the edge of the bed supported by a stool or a chest, like a blanket chest. The woman gets astride him, and lowers herself on to his penis, either facing him or with her back to him. When she has guided the penis into the vagina, she sits down on his upper thighs. If she is facing him she rocks backwards and forwards as I described above, or if with her back to him, she supports her hands on the chest or stool and raises her buttocks up and down. Her feet should be firmly on the ground both for frontal and rear entry, and this prevents her from getting tired. The man does not move at all, but should concentrate on using both hands to stimulate her either about the breast or clitoris or vaginal entrance in the front position; while in the rear entry he should place a hand on each buttock and assist her gently as she goes up and down. This gives her very worthwhile sensations.

If you use any of the positions which are performed on a chair, see that the chair is low enough so that both you and your partner can place your feet firmly on the ground. It might be worth it to adapt a sturdy chair to the right height by cutting off a portion of the legs.

Personally I do not recommend rear entry on the chair. However, if you do decide to use it see that the woman's feet are firmly supported by the floor. In my opinion, the best rear-entry position for the past-middle-aged is the standing one, in which the wife leans forward supporting herself on a table or ledge with her hands, and the husband stands behind her. Maybe she will have to stand on a low stool or a box, which should be absolutely firm and be wide enough for her to stand with her legs slightly apart, to obtain the most comfortable adjustment for differences in height. I would not advise using the rear-entry position in which the woman kneels on the bed or floor and leans forward with her head supported on her arms. The man has to kneel behind her, and this can be quite fatiguing if the man has to adjust his height – as happens in nearly every case – in order to make an effective entry.

Well, there you are! Now it's up to you. These are only a few suggestions. You should experiment, and what is most important, be bold in your experiments. And I wish you the best of luck.

By the way, I am often asked what is the best position in which to perform the manouvre which is commonly called sixty-nine, in which the partners apply mouth-genital caresses to one another simultaneously. Most authorities suggest that this should be done lying on the side, head to toe, with mouth and genitals aligned as this is not at all tiring. Personally, I find the following less exacting and much more satisfactory.

The man lies on his back, with his feet towards the head of the bed and his head a little more than half-way down. The woman places herself above him, with her genital area over his face and her face towards his feet. He places his hands on her buttocks and gently brings her genital area down until he can reach it with tongue and mouth. She will find his genital area within easy reach of her mouth and tongue. If she will keep in the position into which he guides her, he can remove his hands from her buttocks and slip them between their bodies to her breasts, both of whose nipples he will stimulate together. She must be careful not to lie too closely upon him, otherwise she will suffocate him.

You are now equipped to start your new lease of sex, but though I have made some fairly detailed suggestions, it is really up to you to use your imaginations. Remember, sex is a reciprocal arrangement, a partnership which is more clearly defined than probably any other aspect of the whole partnership of marriage. I hope you will find what I have set out here useful.

I hope you will read on, because I have one or two things still to say which may be of help to you from time to time.

7 : Some Questions Answered

As I am devoting this chapter mostly to things medical, I want to begin it with a warning: if you have anything wrong with your sexual apparatus, do consult your doctor. You may have seen from time to time advertisements for this and that pill or tonic, which claim to be able to restore your failing sexual powers. Don't you believe it! Most of these nostrums are the concoctions of quacks. They won't do you any harm, nor will they do you any good. They are a sheer waste of money, and their failure to live up to their promise brings great disappointment to a large number of people who have been foolish enough to be taken in by them. Though I have been encouraging you throughout this book to be bold, to experiment and be adventurous in your sex, nevertheless, take it from me, sex is not something to tinker with. If you have any organic trouble particularly, or think you have, only the best advice can bring you any relief that is possible - and that means authentic medical advice.

Now let me deal with one or two specific questions which frequently rise in regard to sex.

Sex and Sexual Operations

There are two major operations affecting the sexual apparatus which are, or seem to be, becoming increasingly common. One affects the man – prostatectomy; the other affects the woman, hysterectomy, with or without ovarian section.

Prostatectomy

Let me run over briefly what I have already said about the prostate.

The prostate is a large walnut-shaped gland which surrounds

the neck of the bladder in males. (Women do not have a prostate.) It contains numerous other glands which produce the prostatic fluid, which mixes with the fluid produced by the seminal vesicles, into which the semen has moved from the testicles. Together seminal fluid, prostatic fluid and sperms make semen.

As well as being a gland, the prostate also has the qualities of a muscle. When the man begins his orgasm, the muscle-like prostate begins to contract and relax, and forces the semen along the urethra. where it is then taken over by the muscles surrounding the bulb of the penis – that part which lies inside the body – and forces it out of the penis. It is because this occurs by contractions of the various muscles that the semen leaves the penis in spurts.

If a man goes without making love for a long period, some of the prostatic fluid hardens and remains in the gland, which in time becomes enlarged. During the war, I was a prisoner of the Gestapo in Frankfurt-am-Main prison for two years. During this time, as I was on a starvation diet, I lost all sexual desire, and though I did not try to provoke one, I did not have a single erection or orgasm. As a result, in 1965, twenty-two years later, I had to have a prostatectomy.

The necessity to have this operation, in which a large part of the prostate is removed, is brought about by the fact that as it grows larger it closes the outlet of the bladder, making urinating very difficult, setting up all kinds of inflammation in the bladder and ducts, and can become so serious that sooner or later, if not attended to, it could prevent the passing of urine altogether and the consequent death of the patient.

The operation is a major one, and has various after-effects, which in some men cause a good deal of worry in anticipation. In the kind of enlargement caused by hardening of the prostatic fluid – which accounts for the greater part of the cases requiring prostatectomy – only part of the prostate is removed. The rest continues to function both as gland and muscle. It is because this is not understood by so many men that it makes them anxious lest they should be overtaken by the necessity to have the operation performed on them. They are afraid that after had the operation they will be unable to have any further sexual experience.

This is quite wrong. I have found that I achieve orgasm just as easily as I have always done, that the sensations of coming off are, if anything, even more intense than before, though I have always had very intense orgasmic experience, and that my sex-drive has in no way deteriorated. The only difference is that no semen is ejaculated from my penis.

This lack of visible semen is brought about by the fact that, although the seminal vesicles continue to produce their fluid, as does the remainder of the prostate, the muscle quality of the prostate is weakened to the extent that though it in no way interferes with the orgasm sensations, it cannot force the semen down the urethra, and it flows back into the bladder. If you urinate just after coming, you will see semen floating in the urine, that is, if you use a glass receptacle. This is what we call retrograde ejaculation. I have called it semen, but in fact there are no sperms in it, for most, if not all surgeons, for reasons of infection, at the same time that they perform a prostatectomy also carry out the sterilisation technique known as vasectomy, which I have mentioned earlier.

This loss of fertility should not worry any man, because as a rule you are in your late fifties or middle sixties before a prostatectomy becomes necessary, by which time you will probably have had all the children you have planned. I found that the absence of visible semen required a little psychological re-adjustment; but it was not difficult; and now I am glad because I have all the fun of sex without any of the mess.

I think that men also worry because thay know that sometimes a prostatectomy is necessary because the prostate has developed cancer. Fortunately in Great Britain, at all events, cancer of the prostate is responsible for far and away fewer prostatectomies than hardening of the prostatic fluid.

On the other hand, any irritation of the urethra and difficulty in urinating should send you hurrying to the doctor. If caught in time, a large number of malignant prostate growths can be dealt with successfully. If the whole prostate has to be removed, impotence will follow more likely than not.

But for the vast majority of men, there is no reason why their experience should not equal mine; and mine I like.

Hysterectomy

Hysterectomy is the removal by surgery of the womb, which is also accompanied by the removal of one ovary, and sometimes both.

The ovaries have a tendency to develop cysts and other irregularities which give rise to great discomforts and complaints. This usually happens in the five to ten years preceding the menopause and during the menopause. If an operation is necessary to remove either one or both of the ovaries to eliminate the cyst trouble, most surgeons also remove the womb while they are about it. Most surgeons, too, even in cases requiring surgery on both ovaries, try to leave part of one ovary at least, so that the woman's sex hormone continues to be manufactured naturally.

This is possible in the majority of cases, so that while hysterectomy means that the woman will thereafter be sterile, her sex-drive will in no way be affected, and she will be as capable of coming off after it as she was before, if not more so. Even when both ovaries have to be completely removed, injections of the female sex hormone can replace the lack of natural production and she will still experience the need for love-making and be capable of orgasm.

So no woman need fear that either ovarian section or hysterectomy spells the end of her sex-life, for her experience of love-making is in no way diminished.

The womb, equally with the ovaries, also develops tumours and other obstructions which require the removal of the whole organ. If the ovaries are found to be perfectly healthy, when the surgeon comes to examine them, he leaves them intact. In this case, there is no impairment of the enjoyment of sex at all.

Removal of the womb often has the effect of shortening the vagina. First coupling after the operation should therefore be undertaken with the greatest care. If the penis, which before could be accommodated with complete comfort, now causes pain, then shortening has taken place. After a time it may return to its former lengthwise elasticity; but if not the husband will quickly learn to come to terms with the new dimensions. I do not believe I need go into ways and means here; only the dumbest of husbands could fail to work it out for himself.

Sex and the Coronary

Coronary thrombosis is now one of the biggest killers of men in this country and many others. Unfortunately younger and younger men seem to be falling a victim to it, as the stresses of life increase with the passing of every year.

In the past, the sex-life of a man who has had a coronary has been deemed to be over to all intents and purposes, though in the cases of a small thrombosis normality has almost been completely restored. For the remainder, however, the sexual outlook was pretty grim, especially if the patient was in or approaching his senior years.

In America in recent years, however, a change in approach has been receiving attention. Eminent heart-surgeons are wondering whether or not the frustration placed upon coronary patients by forbidding them sex altogether is not, in the long run, more harmful than allowing them to make love. I have been unable to discover any general trend along the same lines in Great Britain's medical circles.

The Americans are insisting, however, that any love-making shall be within the bounds set out by them. The least tiring positions and accessory activities which place the smallest possible strain on the heart meet with their approval, but they insist that love shall be made according to their prescriptions. Since this is clearly better than no love-making at all, the patient would be foolish indeed to ignore expert medical advice, and would do so at his peril. Perhaps in the near future we shall see an extension of the American viewpoint to other countries.

Impotence

Throughout this book I have referred to impotence, the man's inability to achieve an erection, and so be unable to couple. There is no doubt that so far as the sex-life of the man is concerned, this is his greatest fear, from the moment that he becomes aware of the delights his phallus will bring him, as well as *the* means of fulfilling his manhood in reproduction, to the day he dies, or for some other reason gives up all interest in sex, though this is very rare.

As I have remarked before, as a man grows older, his sex-drive loses some of its frequency, and his capacity for strong and sustained erection becomes slightly impaired. It is when he notices that this is taking place that he begins to fear the worst, though in the vast majority of cases his fear is groundless.

Certainly, by far the larger number of cases of organic impotence occur in older men, but even so this kind of impotence is comparatively rare, which is just as well; for though miracles have been performed with the help of hormone injections, there is a fairly high proportion of cases which stubbornly refuse to respond to any treatment. It is, however, temporary impotence which is the main cause of the fear, and the fear feeds the impotence whether the primary cause is psychological or organic.

At the first sign of repeated inability to achieve erection, see a doctor. If he finds there is nothing organically wrong with your sexual apparatus, then the causes are psychological and are capable of being treated and removed.

Again, as I have pointed out earlier, in quite a number of cases the temporary impotence which has psychological roots has been found to spring from the fact that in later life it is the woman who seems to have, and very often has, the stronger sex-drive. And it is this which can be seen to be the direct cause of the man's failure. Many men, finding they are no longer in control of an aspect of their married lives in which they have most of their time been master, build up an unconscious resentment and frustration against their new secondary role. This is often, as I have tried to explain, enough to take away all interest in sex. If it does not do this, then it leads to temporary impotence.

In order to attain the greatest heights in sexual pleasure the mind must be free of distracting influences. The uppermost thing in the man's mind when he becomes sexually active must be his desire for the other person involved. Every successful act of love-making and coupling for the man requires the full co-ordination of almost all of his forces - psychic, nervous, glandular and muscular. The failure of any one of these functions will diminish or destroy potency, which may be caused by a variety of strong emotional reactions such as animosity, fear, anger, disgust or anxiety.

As another cause, it is possible for a man at this point in his life to suffer from discontent and regret over the scale of his life's achievements and goals he has failed to reach. If he takes these feelings and preoccupations into his love-bed with him the result is nearly always impotence.

One of the greatest tragedies of impotence is that of a man, having 'failed' once, is ever after in dread of failing again – and, more often than not, he does just that. It is ironical that the fear of impotence is the most frequent cause of impotence.

Another common cause of fear lies in the superstition that the 'change' in men marks the end of sexual relations. Let the angle of their erections decline by so much as a few degrees and they are thrown into a panic, foreseeing the end of their potency. They may even go so far as to cease all love-making, because they are convinced that this is what Nature means they should do.

What then, if anything, can be done to prevent or cure psychological impotence?

Here as in all other instances the saying 'An ounce of prevention is worth a pound of cure' holds true. For that man whose impotence may be caused by the fear that the 'change' means the end of sexual usefulness, the knowledge that this is totally untrue may do the trick and release him from his complex. *There is no biological event, except the onset of disease and death, that marks the end of pleasurable sex-life.*

The problem is simply that the middle-aged man who becomes unduly conscious of his waning sexual capacity creates his own emotional crisis. When he reaches the years of relatively infrequent love-making, he views his youthful potency with nostalgia. But what is he measuring himself against, against what standards of performance? The youth of eighteen who was capable of coming eighteen times a week? But this is a fairy-tale picture he is evoking. If he recalls those years correctly they were likely to be years of flash-point erotics. The years of sweet, long-drawn-out love-making with his wife were still in the future. There was nothing enriching about his attempts at sex then.

Such a man would not dream of measuring his business or professional powers or his value as a citizen against his eighteen-year-old self. In these respects he has accumulated maturity and wisdom, not to mention subtle skills, and ingenuity. Why then should he assume that in sex alone maturity is without value?

In a proper frame of mind there is no reason why he cannot lead a rich and fulfilling sexual life for many years to come.

For centuries rejuvenation has been one of the dream-fantasies of mankind, but it was suspected only fairly recently that in reality we carried much of the power for this in our minds. If there is any rule for combating impotence, it is most probably – in fact, it is certainly – a determination to go on being interested in love and love-making and doing both for as long as possible.

In our sexual lives, memory, conditioning and experience play a role whose importance we are only just beginning to understand. Deeply satisfying, deeply emotional relationships store up a positive charge of energy which our bodies continue to draw on for many years. Erotic experiences in early and middle years cast their happiness before them. The quality and sharpness of previous conditioning. If the erotic experience of the partners has been good, desire and love-making continue far beyond the norm.

If any of my readers has the misfortune to be suffering from psychological impotence, may I plead with him to try to cure himself quickly, and if he does not succeed within a fairly short time to seek psychiatric advice. I make this plea because his state will have repercussions in every sphere of his life. Not only will he suffer, but also those about him, and his work. It does, perhaps, require a degree of determination and will-power, but the results will justify any trouble to which he is put.

And after all, this suffering is so unnecessary.

8 : Sex To The End

At the risk of repeating myself yet again, I hope I have shown there is no reason at all why most men and women, given normal good health, should not continue to enjoy sex, and derive a great deal of comfort out of it, to the end. It is mainly a matter of getting things into perspective and proportion.

So long as you make love regularly through the years, following the dictates of your desire, it does not matter as time goes by that you should find your frequency becoming progressively less and your orgasms not so intense as they used to be. The real point is, are you relieving your tension when it demands it, and are you feeling satisfied with your orgasm sensations and their aftermath of release? If you are, you should have no complaints on the physical side, provided you are equally convinced that your partner is achieving comparable results with yours.

Remember that impotence is largely in the mind. Tell yourself that it does not exist and it will cease to exist.

Keep your body in trim and don't let it go to seed and fat. Match this general condition with a constant toning up of your sexual apparatus by carrying out regularly the exercises I have suggested, and you will find yourself a happy man in a happy body.

You will also find yourself a happy man with a happy mind. In these later years you have a lifetime's experience of sharing a life behind you. If it has been at all a happy one then you do not need me to tell you that this happiness will be carried over into the years of your sexual tailing-off. Because you can still use love-making to express your love, though it is only occasionally, you will find that the quality of this aged love is something you would not earlier have believed could exist. Love of both kinds will give you a tranquillity that is so fitting to the climax of old-age. Serenity has a price that is above rubies. This makes any effort you have to sustain to refurbish and renew your love and your experience of sex, as the great opportunity middle-age gives you to do so pale into insignificance beside the results you cannot help but achieve.

9 : Left Alone!

I feel I cannot end this book without a word to those who find themselves left alone towards the end of their lives through the loss of their partner. Because they are left on their own, this does not mean that their sexual desires have died also. What are they to do unless they are to marry again, and this many have no intention of doing?

I hope neither elderly men nor women will hesitate to use the one outlet they have. If it is physically and psychologically natural for adolescents to masturbate, then it must be equally right and proper for adults deprived of the natural outlet of intercourse to use the same means of relieving their tensions.

I do not think this will present a problem for many men, but for women it may present some problems of morals and behaviour. On this I would like to quote from an article in *The Encyclopedia of Sexual Behaviour*[1] by Dr Lester W. Dearborn. He writes: 'I recently had a female client of seventy-three who came because she was worried over the fact that she masturbated two or three times a week. She reported that she had had a very happy marriage, that her husband had died five years earlier, and that since then she had had to turn to masturbation. She wanted to know if I could recommend some doctor who could give her medicine to prevent this. She was obviously embarrassed to have to admit masturbation and felt there was something wrong with a woman of her age so indulging.

'I tried to quiet her fears and told her that I knew of no method of treatment that would be of any use, and that most of the doctors with whom I was acquainted would not feel that there was need for any treatment. I told her that she should

[1] The Corsano Company Ltd, London, 1961.

accept auto-erotic release as a perfectly proper outlet and not worry about it, especially as she led a very active life, took care of her home, worked outside, had social commitments, and seemed to have adjusted herself to widowhood very well indeed – provided she could get rid of the notion that in having sex desires and needing an outlet there was something wrong with her.

So don't worry if you find you must seek this kind of relief for your desires. It is not a disgraceful nor yet an undignified thing for a widow or divorcee to need the consolation of sex at whatever age she may be, and if masturbation is the only outlet she has, why should she deprive herself of it? She is doing no one any harm, and herself a good deal of good.

10 : Cases

The case-histories which I am presenting here I have selected because they are typical of the various categories into which my correspondents have naturally fallen. You have the couple of fifty plus who have been happily married for a quarter of a century or more, who have developed a satisfactory sex-life in the early years of their marriage and are having no trouble with sex in middle-age; and you have the couple who have more or less dropped out from sex, who are bitter about it, but who have only themselves to blame because they were too lazy or too gentlemanly or ladylike to treat sex seriously and light-heartedly at the same time, so that it has meant nothing special to them and has become a bore; and so on. In reading them you will, I think, readily perceive the goal to aim for, the pitfalls to avoid in your own coming to terms with sex after forty.

Case P

The Ps are both fifty; they have been married for twenty-six years, and have three children. Two still live at home, and one is still being educated. P is a senior lecturer in a university, working from nine to four; Mrs P is a housewife.

At nine-and-a-half stone P, for his age and height - five feet ten - is somewhat under-weight. Mrs P, who is only five feet three and weighs ten stone, is about right, though perhaps a pound or two over the average. But the point is that neither of them has gone to seed physically.

P's hobbies are fishing, painting and writing; Mrs P's painting and dog-breeding. Twice a month they have friends in to dinner. Once a week they to to the cinema, and go on frequent walks together with the dogs.

P smokes twelve to fifteen cigarettes daily, and has a pint of beer. The health of both of them is excellent; they take no drugs or 'pills' of any kind.

When they were first married, they often made love daily, and never less than four times a week. Now they have sex once a week, which they find about right. P still has a strong erection. though sometimes he has a slight difficulty in obtaining one, He does not require his wife's assistance, however. He has had no operation which might have a bearing on this.

To begin with he experienced some difficulty in controlling his progress to orgasm, and this had some bearing on the length of time they devoted to their love-making. Now they make love for twenty minutes or so, the length of time being determined by the wife in reaching orgasm. Mrs P, by the way, has not yet completed the menopause, and has had no operation on her sexual apparatus.

They have always used a fair variety of sexual caresses, including cunnilingus and fellatio. At the beginning Mrs P had some difficulty coming off, a difficulty which lasted for the first ten years, chiefly because neither of them appreciated the importance of clitoral stimulation. On this P says, 'My wife has never been able to have orgasm in intercourse or even through clitoral stimulation by me, though she enjoys these. After ten years of marriage she discovered she could bring about her orgasm for herself and since then our love-making has been built round that situation.' By these means Mrs P has mastered the art of multiple-orgasm, and also has five or six orgasms to P's one, her maximum being fifteen in one session.

P goes on, 'Love-making starts with kissing, breast fondling and some manipulation of her vagina by me. She is always extremely wet and ready. I then suck her nipples and perhaps her clitoris, and presently put on a sheath and have intercourse in my own time (usually five minutes or so). I then move over and, after a little more kissing she uses her hand to bring on her orgasm by rubbing her clitoris. This first climax may take her ten minutes to obtain and is invariably followed at quite short intervals by further climaxes brought on by continued rnbbing of the clitoris. While she is doing this, I may suck her nipples.

'Usually she is satisfied after four of five orgasms in this way, and after some further kissing we go to sleep. Occasionally she may be specially roused and want more – say eight or nine times.

'This would happen more usually just after a period or after reading an erotic book or seeing a film. Also, we both have occasional fantasies which we act out in our bedroom, and these generate considerable excitement even now. These include, in my case, making love to her rather roughly while she is in her underclothes. In her case she sometimes asks me to masturbate while she watches closely.'

For their coupling, besides the face-to-face-man-above, they use woman-above-kneeling and squatting, and rear-entry-woman-kneeling. As far as I can gather they have never used woman-above-prone or made love on a chair, though they 'quite often "play about" (feeling) in a friendly horseplay manner, say in the kitchen' and have occasionally made love in the kitchen and sitting-room. They like to allow about an hour for their love-making. Sometimes she takes the initiative throughout, but he does not really care for this, preferring to take the initiative himself.

They are clearly a happy and contented couple, well adjusted to one another, appreciative of one another's special needs, and all set for a happy sex-life into old-age.

Case H

H is fifty-seven and Mrs H is fifty-two; they have been married for thirty-two years, and have three children, one of whom, who is still at school, lives at home.

H is a professional man, his working week being approximately thirty-eight hours. During term time Mrs H helps with school meals. About once a month they have a few friends in 'for wine, coffee and conversation' and every three or four weeks they go out to dinner, or the theatre or visit friends.

H's hobbies are do-it-yourself jobs about the house, attending learned societies, a little writing and lecturing, which Mrs H matches with gardening and knitting.

At five feet six, which is also Mrs H's height, H's weight, at ten-and-a-half stone, is about right, so is her weight at just over nine stone. They are not drinkers, though they enjoy a glass of wine, and he smokes about five cigarettes a day. He described his health as 'reasonably good for age', but he is liable to back trouble if he undertakes heavy lifting. Mrs H has had outstandingly good health, but is now facing a uterine operation. They do not take any drugs or 'pills'.

They have made love four or five times a week throughout their married life up to now. On this H says, 'In our early years we thought it was weakening to have it more than about four times a week, and also I was in a heavy manual job and used to get tired. Also again, we were sold on "modern" literature saying a woman ought to come off every time, and trying to achieve this was a very exhausting, not to say fruitless, procedure. We are now back to the same frequency, but in many of the years between kept to about thirteen times a fortnight for months on end. We also discovered that menstruation, except for the first day, was no bar.' He would still like to have sex six or seven times a week, if he followed his sex-drive promptings, and says that he is only prevented from doing so by 'lack of steam in the engine', though I am not clear what he means.

He has no difficulty with his erections, and has had no operation. He has had no difficulty in controlling his progress to coming, and if he alone is to come they spend five or ten minutes on their love-making whereas if she is to come, too, about half an hour. Mrs H, by the way, has completed the menopause.

In the early days they had not discovered clitoral stimulation, and consequently there was some difficulty in bringing Mrs H off. In fact their caresses were limited to the breasts and kissing. Now they have discovered clitoral stimulation and use it most of the time according to needs. He makes the following interesting comment on this: 'It is not in her to come off more than three or four times a month, and probably no woman can come off every time unless intercourse is infrequent. The "difficulty" was that nothing would rouse her to orgasm.' (Not that he had used cunnilingus on her, which might have turned out to be the touch-paper.) He explains further: 'In the early days we failed to get any arousal out of the clitoris. Either it had too thick a skin or there was a psychological blockage. Not until after she had three children did we eventually get the clitoris to respond.' This seems to have prevented them from becoming adventurous in their love-making, which I think was more largely due to Mrs H's nonconformist upbringing. For example, he has asked her to fellate him but she has refused. On this he comments: 'I think almost all women are conditioned against eroticism by their upbringing. I would very much like to have introduced variety into our love-making but my wife refused. Yet she is more sexy and more accommodating than most married women, and our marriage, based on sex, has been a successful one. We have worked out a *modus vivendi*, whereby she will almost always "submit" to my "lust" for the vicarious pleasure of satisfying me, and I for my part will take the trouble, and it is often very tedious, of playing with her for up to thirty minutes to bring her off.

'I am absolutely convinced that a woman who has had children will not come off on the majority of sex occasions, unless these are very infrequent.' (This of course is not true.)

I think his future sex-life, if there is to be one, will have to be very carefully handled, unless Mrs H is content to go on being influenced by her nonconformist upbringing to the extent of rarely co-operating and yet prepared to let him have his pleasure. But this I believe will pall for him after a time, and just at the time when co-operative sex should be the mainstay of the relationship.

Case D

The case of the Ds is in sharp contrast with the Hs. As soon as you begin to read their replies you can sense that here is a really sexually happy couple and hence a completely contented couple.

D is fifty-five, Mrs D fifty-one, and they have been married thirty years. They have three children; the youngest, the son, is still at his university. Between them they run two shops.

They entertain neighbours to drinks and have members of the family to meals. Twice a year they give a large party. D had a heart attack six years ago, and since then they have not gone out much, but they have two or three holidays together in the year. He is interested in politics, literature, the theatre and watching tennis, and is a keen motorist. Mrs D shares these interests.

At ten stone four D is not overweight for his five feet ten; nor is Mrs D, who is five feet five, at eight-and-a-half stone. He smokes twenty-five cigarettes a day, and drinks very moderately.

At the time of his heart attack it was discovered that he had a heart tremor. He also has a tendency to ulcer trouble and heavy colds, but otherwise is 'full of energy'. Heroin has been prescribed for his heart condition.

When first married, they made love every day. Now they make love three times in ten days. He would like to more often, but he is away from home two nights a week, and his wife works very hard on the last three days of the week. He feels that the ideal programme would be to make love three nights consecutively and then wait five or six days.

He has strong erections and needs no help from his wife. Mrs D is going through the menopause.

They have been fairly adventurous in their love-making, though they no longer use mouth-genital caresses. She has occasional multiple-orgasm. On holiday they like to make love during the day; they would do so at home, but their house is a busy place. They have made love in the sitting-room and bathroom, and outdoors in the woods. He has a slight tendency to premature ejaculation, and cannot receive any stimulation from her. Very occasionally Mrs D takes the initiative and follows through to orgasm.

They have always been able to discuss sex frankly between themselves and with their children.

D made the following general comments: 'Many people we know no longer have any sex. As they are in our age group it is incredible. Nearly always they have single beds or separate rooms. We find when on holiday in hotels if we have single rooms we fuck less often. (We use the word and always have for the act – my wife hates it to be used in any other connotation.) Both at Easter and Whitsun we had a double bed and made love every night. After Easter my wife booked for Whitsun and insisted on having the same room. This pleased me knowing that I had pleased her. This was when we were relaxed on holiday after good meals and pleasant drinks.

'We inevitably wake up intertwined in the morning, and my wife feeling my erection says "We're feeling healthy today", and we make plans for the day and frequently for the night. If I have not got an erection she insists that I take it easy during the day, switches my appointments and thus makes it a closer relationship. One feels marvellous after a really beautiful fuck and to get out of the habit must deaden your middle-age.'

Case L

The case of the Ls is interesting, chiefly on account of Mrs L's approach to sex. Both are sixty-four and they have been married thirty-eight years. He is a retired accountant. They do not go out much together. He watches a good deal of cricket, which Mrs L does not like. Neither is overweight. Before he had angina fifteen years ago he used to smoke sixty-five cigarettes a day, now he smokes only three a week. He drinks very moderately. Drugs are prescribed for his heart condition and asthma.

When they were first married they used to make love twice a week; now they do it once a week. He would like a higher frequency, but Mrs L will not co-operate.

He does not have very strong erections, but there is no organic damage, for his morning erections are vigorous. They were never very adventurous in their love-making and coupling; and are even less so now, when he has a tendency to premature ejaculation.

They always make love in the mornings nowadays, and spend about ten minutes from beginning to end. He would like her to fondle his penis and fellate him. He has told her so, but she has refused as she finds both repugnant.

Once every two months or so, she takes the initiative through orgasm, and though this pleases him, she does not care much for it. She finds kissing most stimulating, and wishes he would kiss her more, and has told him so, but 'he can't wait – he always comes first. I rarely want it nowadays, and certainly do not wish he would make love more often! I think sex is unbecoming for a woman over fifty. I might like sex more if he didn't come so quickly always. . . .'

If L ever reads this, and recognises his 'case', may I ask him to get in touch with me through my publisher. I think I can make some suggestion which would help with his premature ejaculation.

Case O

Both the Os work from nine to five. He is fifty-three and she is fifty-two. They have been married twenty-three years and have no children. They entertain quite a lot at home, and go out a good deal, chiefly to the theatre. Their hobbies are reading, the theatre and walking. Neither of them is overweight, and they are roughly the same height – five feet four. They smoke ten to fifteen cigarettes a day, and like a glass or two of wine a day. Their health is 'reasonably good'. He takes no drugs of any sort, but she takes antihistamin for an allergy.

When they were first married they made love daily; now they do it twice a week. He would like to double this frequency, but she is often too tired.

He has no erection trouble and does not need his wife to stimulate him in order to bring one on. He has no difficulty in controlling his pace towards orgasm and she has no difficulty in coming. She is going through the menopause.

They have been moderately adventurous in their love-making and coupling and clearly have a repertoire on which they can ring the changes, so there is no sign of boredom. She frequently has multiple-orgasm. They used to use face-to-face and rear-entry on their sides, 'but we have given these up now as they are too strenuous'. They have always made a practice of making love at other times of the day, generally in the afternoons, and still do so once in ten days. They also make love in the sitting-room on a divan or the floor with the same frequency. They spend about three-quarters of an hour on their love-making. They always make love naked in bed, partially clothed in the sitting-room and elswhere.

O says, 'Technique varies. Usually my wife has her back towards me while I have my arm round her and caress her breasts. I then run my hand down towards her pubic zone and caress her vaginal area. I will then push my penis between her legs and with this stroke her outer lips. When she is ready to receive me, she will turn and I will then proceed to have sexual intercourse. Sometimes I will withdraw and go down on her – after which I will resume sexual intercourse to orgasm. While I am stroking her outer lips with my penis, she will stroke my testicles, and put her arm behind me and stroke my buttocks. During actual intercourse, she will kiss and bite my shoulders and chest and dig her nails into my back. We have always used sixty-nine through to orgasm on occasion, but don't do it so frequently now as we did.'

The Os, I think, will have a happy sex-life in their old-age, and will not make the same unhappy picture as the Gs.

Case G

G is seventy-seven, Mrs G seventy-two. They have been married twenty-one years, and have no children as Mrs G had completed her menopause when they married. They entertain a little, mostly relations, and go out together. His hobbies are music, politics, and reading; she has no hobbies 'but is very socially minded'. They are vegetarians, and are underweight for their age. He makes his own cigarettes and smokes a pipe, and they drink very little.

When first married they made love about once a month. For the past four years they have not made love at all, though he would like to once a week, but she is not interested.

He still has quite strong erections and requires no stimulation from his wife to bring one on. They have been fairly adventurous in their techniques, which included cunnilingus, and she always came easily, which was just as well as he has had a tendency to premature ejaculation. Despite this, he claims, 'My wife has always been rather frigid. We never discussed sex. She left it all to me. We have never made love except with me above, always did it at night and always in bed.

'My wife is not very interested in sex. I should like to discuss it, but it would embarrass her. I have very strong sexual desires and feel very frustrated. I should like extra-marital relations, but do not know how to set about it at my age. It may interest you to know that I have never seen a woman's sex organs. We have always made love in the dark, and I have never seen her undressed, and only within the last few years did I learn the sex technique. The hush-hush taboo on sex is very annoying to me, although the younger generation seem less inhibited. I think the sex act for a man is the nearest approach to ecstasy that is possible from a physical point of view, although it is so brief. In my case the knowledge I have acquired has come too late. Neither my wife nor myself had any instruction in sex matters when we were children and consequently it was invested with an aura of shame.'

All of which I find very sad, and sincerely hope that none of my readers will condemn themselves to a similar fate.

SEX MANNERS FOR MEN

A unique and outspoken guide to lovemaking

by Robert Chartham

How to be both Husband and Lover. The techniques that every husband should know to please his wife.

In SEX MANNERS FOR MEN Robert Chartham, a marriage guidance counsellor, approaches this vital topic in a personal and confidential way. He uses his own experience to discuss the art of sex and the ways of love, including its most intimate vocabulary.

His frank, liberating views dispel many false attitudes and inhibitions about sex and show men how to become successful lovers.

NEW ENGLISH LIBRARY 25p